Stefan Dramiński

The Heavy Cruiser Lützow

KAGERO

The heavy cruiser *Lützow*, starboard side, July 1942.

In the aftermath of the First World War the German fleet had been left without all worthful ships, and there was nothing at first to indicate that the force would be revived. Despite the restraints imposed, it was not long before engineering work on heavy vessels was underway. The first warship of the new type was named *Deutschland*. With rather unconventional technical specifications, she could not be easily and explicitly classified within a definite category of ships. The *Deutschland*'s service was long and intensive. Later on, during the course of the Second World War, both her name and classification were changed to *Lützow* and heavy cruiser respectively.

The stipulations of the Treaty of Versailles that allowed Germany to retain a fleet of only six battleships and as many light cruisers in addition to twelve torpedo boats and as many torpedo boat destroyers came into effect on January 10, 1920. In 1922 five powers became signatories to the Washington Naval Treaty, on whose authority the German navy could replace the eight old battleships (including two in reserve) it had after World War I with new constructions. The displacement of the new warships was not, however, to exceed 10,000 tons. Two years after the treaty was signed, Germany started development of a future battleship under the contract name *Ersatz Preussen* which would enter service as a replacement for the reserve battleship *Preussen*.

The new vessel was envisaged in two ways. One view premised development of a warship for defensive tasks. This construction would feature armament of a power inversely proportional to the speed. The premise of the other view was a construction classified between the battleship and the cruiser. This ship would be armed with six 28cm guns and eight 12cm ones. Fitted with two Diesel engines rated at 54,000 horsepower, she would attain speeds of up to 28 knots. Such a construction would make the ship effective in combat against cruisers while the high speeds would make her fast enough to overtake battleships. Initially, the naval authorities were inclined toward the former, more traditional concept. However, in June of 1927 *Admiral* Zenker, commander-in-chief of the Reichsmarine, changed his mind and supported the development of a warship based on the other construction.

The designing stage allowed development of two ships, "A" and "B", unconventionally classified as *Panzerschiffe*, or literally "armored ships". They were later commonly called battleships while the English-speaking countries used the term "pocket battleships". When planning a budget for the year 1928, though, the higher chamber of the German parliament did not approve funding for initial construction of the "A" ship, justifying the refusal with the horrendous state of the Reich's finances. The case ended up with the lower chamber, the *Reichstag*, who approved the project on March 27, 1928. The polemic over spending money for naval armament had taken almost a year. It was not until a memorial by the Reich's minister of defense—in which he argued for the necessity to defend communication with East Prussia in the event of war with Poland or France—that the opposition yielded and the project could be approved.

The ship's keel was laid on February 5, 1929. The Reichsmarine had signed the contract for building the vessel with the German shipyard Deutsche Werke AG of Kiel. The celebratory launching of the ship's hull took place more than two years later, on May 19, 1931. Apart from a numerous audience of approximately 60,000 observers, the official ceremony was attended by the Reich's president Paul von Hindenburg and the chancellor Heinrich Brüning. During Brüning's speech the ship began to unexpectedly slide down the slipway. A bottle of champagne was broken over the bow at the very last moment, thus concluding the christening of the battleship by the name of *Deutschland*.

A construction outline

As has already been mentioned, the leading premise of the design work on the warship was the fitting of possibly heavy guns and a power unit capable of reaching significantly high speeds while at the same time keeping displacement relatively low at around 10,000 tons.

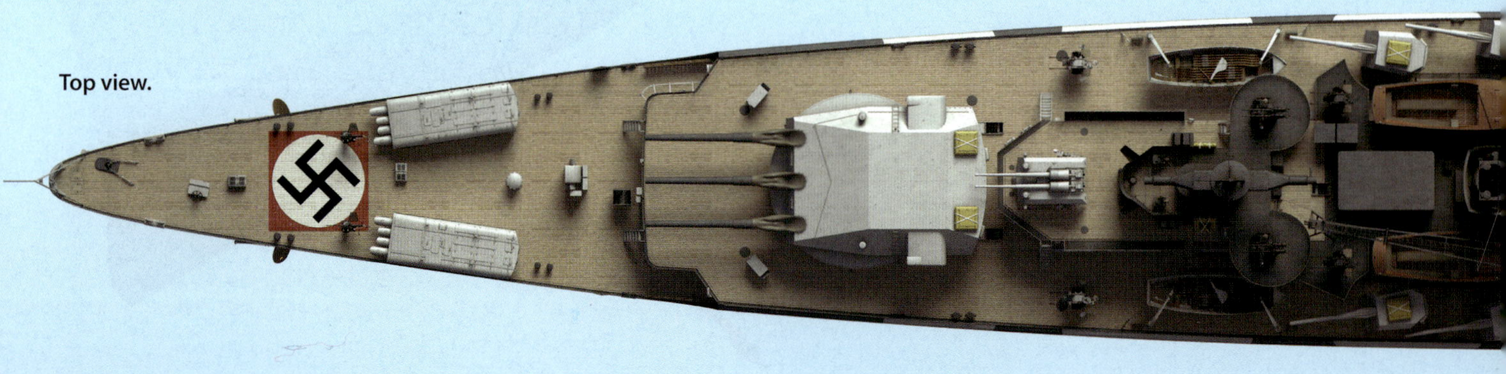

Top view.

To reach these objectives necessarily required making considerable savings in the tonnage area. That was achieved at the expense of the armor, which was not very solid: on the main belt it was 80mm at the thickest part whereas on the main deck it was 45mm.

The ship was propelled by eight Diesel engines manufactured by MAN that allowed her to attain the speed of up to 28 knots at 48,390 horsepower. Range was impressive, ensuring no less than 17,400 miles of travel at a fuel-efficient speed of 13 knots. Still, the choice of the compression-ignition units proved to be inexpedient, as the ship would be troubled by frequent breakdowns in the future.

The armament, on the other hand, was very strong. The main artillery consisted of six 28cm guns in two triple turrets (one at the bow and one at the stern). A secondary battery of eight 15cm guns was mounted at single positions amidships and arranged four per side. This was complemented by anti-aircraft weapons: three 8.8cm guns, eight 3.7cm guns and eight 2cm ones. Because of an increasing threat of aerial fire, the anti-aircraft battery would later be modified and reinforced on multiple occasions. The ship also carried torpedo armament, with two quadruple 53.3cm launchers installed at the stern.

Early service and the Spanish Civil War

The outfitting work was carried out until November of 1932. In January of the following year the battleship underwent her first sea trials. On completion of propulsion system tests and after artillery trials, she was commissioned into the Reichsmarine on April 1, 1933, where command of the ship was taken by *Kapitän zur See* Hermann von Fischel.

The *Deutschland*'s maiden voyage began in May of the same year. She departed Wilhelmshaven and, through the Skagerrak, headed for Kiel. This period of time was spent dealing with engine malfunctions and training the crew. Then the *Deutschland* continued on her first voyage, visiting Balholmen in Norway, the Faroe Islands and Iceland. When in the Skagerrak waters, she took part in a modest ceremony held in remembrance of the people killed in the Battle of Jutland. The battleship returned to Wilhelmshaven on June 1. After some engine defects had been removed on the ship, the *Deutschland* set out again on June 6, now for the Baltic Sea, in order to conduct speed trials and artillery tests. She was eventually declared ready for active naval service on December 10, 1933.

Early in the following year the battleship's crew underwent training, whereupon the ship left Kiel in April. She was headed for Norway and carried the Reich's chancellor Adolf Hitler onboard among others. On return to Kiel in May of the same year, the *Deutschland* participated in fleet exercises in the Baltic Sea. In June she performed artillery drills in the waters of the Atlantic Ocean with assistance from the light cruiser *Köln*. Further maneuvers took the ship to the Swedish port of Göteborg in the autumn. The battleship's cruise continued with a visit to Scotland in October of 1934 as a Reichsmarine flagship. When back from this voyage, the *Deutschland* cast anchor again at the Wilhelmshaven shipyard for maintenance and refitting. The shipyard work was completed by February of the following year.

In March of 1935 the battleship was ready to set out on a voyage to Brazil, Trinidad and Aruba. The focus of this long cruise was engine testing. The *Deutschland* returned to Wilhelmshaven on April 19, having covered more than 12,000 nautical miles at an average speed of 16 knots. On September 30, 1935, the battleship was passed under new command. With *Kapitän zur See* Paul Fanger now in charge, more artillery drills for the *Deutschland* followed in October with a sister battleship, the *Admiral Scheer*. These exercises took place off the Canary Islands and the Azores, and were accompanied by fuel consumption measurements and towing practice. After these maneuvers the battleship underwent thorough maintenance in November of 1935.

The first half of 1936 was generally a period of crew training. Later in May the *Deutschland* participated in a fleet review at Kiel on the anniversary of the Battle of Jutland. This celebration also became an occasion to inaugurate a naval memorial in Laboe dedicated to com-

Port side. In the summer of 1942 the ship wore irregular disruptive camouflage.

The fore superstructure as seen from the back. Air recognition swastikas are painted on both the forecastle and the quarterdeck.

memorate the fallen sailors. From there the battleship sailed through the Bay of Biscay and the Irish Sea on to Copenhagen, where she paid a visit on June 19.

Because of the outbreak of a civil war in Spain, the *Deutschland* was called back in to Wilhelmshaven on July 23 from her torpedo trials being conducted in the Baltic Sea. She was resupplied with ammunition, fuel and food and ordered into Spanish waters along with the sister ship *Admiral Scheer* under the command of *Konteradmiral* Rolf Carls. Both vessels were followed by three other ships: the light cruiser *Köln* and two torpedo boats. The mission objective was to evacuate and provide security to German citizens who were staying in Spain. The actual purpose of the mission, though, was to protect German transport vessels which carried supplies for the nationalists commanded by General Franco. The *Deutschland* arrived at the port of San Sebastian on July 26, 1936. She also made stops at the ports of Bilbao and La Coruña, and afterwards at Cádiz, Almeria and Málaga in early August. On August 3 the *Deutschland* prevented the north-African port of Ceuta from com-

ing under fire from the rebels. During this month she also took part in an escort of freighter ships to Lisbon.

As a result of an agreement signed on August 24, 1936 by four countries: England, France, Germany and Italy, which had established sectors for international control of the Spanish coast, the *Deutschland* was sent back to Germany and returned to Wilhelmshaven on August 30. However, she was redeployed to Spain in October and did not return to her native port in Germany until November 21.

In late January of 1937 the battleship departed Kiel, heading for Spanish waters for a third time. Having finished this operation in the second half of March, the ship was re-docked at Wilhelmshaven, where she underwent a refit. The agreement signed in August of the preceding year came into force in April, whereupon the *Deutschland* left German territory, setting out for Spain for a fourth time on May 10. The ship sailed to Palma on the island of Majorca. The port was hosting a number of other neutral warships as well. On the morning of May 24 the harbor became the target of an aerial attack by the Republican forces, but the battleship remained unscathed.

The *Deutschland* was then hastily ordered out to Ibiza. While cruising off the island on May 29, she came within sight of two Republican cruisers and four destroyers. A moment later there was another sighting, with two enemy aircraft being spotted nearby. Although combat alert was sounded at 1840 hours, it was already too late for the ship. The Soviet-built SB-2 bombers attacked from an altitude of 1000 meters, deploying two 50kg bombs onto the battleship. The first one hit the cover of the third starboard 15cm gun, with the shrapnel penetrating the fuel tank of a floatplane. The resulting fire embraced the aircraft and a boat, and led to an explosion of 15mm rounds. The second bomb struck the main deck, penetrating it near the fore superstructure turret, to blow up inside crew quarters. More than twenty seamen were killed on the spot while eighty others were wounded. The fire spread very quickly and clouds of smoke formed below deck. A torpedo boat, the *Leopard*, came to rescue and began making attempts to extinguish the fire. The situation was back under control by 1930 hours. The attack left a total of 31 people dead while 110 men had sustained injuries, predominantly burns.

On the next day 35 severely wounded crewmen were transported to a hospital in Gibraltar. Thirty-four others with injuries were transferred to land on May 31. On the very same day Hitler issued an order for the *Admiral Scheer* to open retaliatory fire upon the port of Almeria. The fallen sailors were buried with military honors on June 1, 1931. However, upon Hitler's demand the bodies were exhumed and sent home to Germany. The coffins were delivered onboard the *Deutschland* by the British on June 11. The battleship arrived at Wilhelmshaven five days later. The funeral services were held on the day after and were attended by Adolf Hitler himself, other high-ranked national representatives and several thousand citizens. The *Deutschland* was docked for maintenance and refitting.

November 5 saw the battleship return once again to the waters of Spain. She paid visits to ports such as El Ferrol, Cádiz, Tangier, Algeciras, Ceuta and Melilla. In November the *Deutschland* was diverted to Italy, casting anchor at Naples and other places. She headed back for Spanish waters in February of 1938, where she was to remain with a short break until August 15. A week later, on the 22nd, the ship was on parade with the German fleet at Kiel in celebration of the launching of the heavy cruiser *Prinz Eugen*. A month later the *Deutschland* set out for the Atlantic Ocean while Germany was busy negotiating the detachment of a region from Czechoslovakia and its annexation into the Reich.

The battleship came to port at Vigo, Spain, on September 22, from where she headed on for the Canary Islands and the Azores. Along the way she was being tracked by Royal Navy ships, including the battle cruiser *HMS Hood*. Cruising through Santa Cruz, Cádiz, Tangier and Gibraltar, the *Deutschland* returned to Germany. In the period between May of 1933 and the autumn of 1938 the battleship had covered over 130,000 nautical miles.

Towards the end of 1938 the *Deutschland* completed a series of trials in the Baltic Sea. These were followed in February of the following year by artillery drills off the Canary Islands. On March 21, 1939, Adolf Hitler came aboard the ship at Swinemünde[1]. From there, other Kriegsmarine warships accompanied the *Deutschland* on her voyage to Memel[2], a town acquired by the Reich as the result of a German ultimatum. When back at Wilhelmshaven, the ship participated in a parade to celebrate the launching of a newest battleship, the *Tirpitz*. The final pre-war period mostly saw the warship being refitted or in training. After being declared ready for combat, the *Deutschland* departed for Denmark Strait between Greenland and Iceland on August 24, 1939. Taking position in the Atlantic would enable the warship to swiftly commence corsair operations against Allied supply ships in the event of war with Poland.

Wartime operations

The *Deutschland*'s commanding staff received communications about anticipated war operations on August 31, 1939. At that time, it was uncertain how the Western nations would react in the case of Poland's territory being attacked by the Reich. Over the three days that followed, the battleship was being notified about England and France joining an anti-German coalition. Starting on September 3, combat watches were ordered onboard the ship. On September 11, after filling up her fuel tanks from the tanker ship *Westerwald*, the battleship assumed a southerly course. On September 27 the *Deutschland* was granted authorization to commence a raiding mission against French and British sea traffic. Following this, the battleship sank a British cargo ship, the *Stonegate*, off the Bermuda Islands on October 5 (but only after evacuating the latter ship's crew to the battleship). Four days later the *Deutschland* captured an American vessel, the *City of Flint*, which was carrying a cargo to Great Britain. The captured crew was replaced by German crewmen and the ship was dispatched to Germany as a prize. Three more ships were bothered over the following couple of days: Norway's *Jacob Christensen* and the tanker *Kongsdal* were stopped and released after document examination; the Norwegian cargo ship *Lorentz W. Hansen* was sunk during an encounter off Newfoundland.

The *Deutschland* made a failed attempt in late October to fuel up from the supply ship *Westerwald*. Because of a heavy storm the battleship sustained some light damage (including a flooded propulsion system) and was only able to rendezvous a few days later, on the 25th. She was subsequently ordered back to the Reich for engine repairs.

November 16 marked the ship's transfer under a new commander, *Kapitän zur See* August Thiele. Towards the end of the month the battleship accompanied some cruisers and destroyers on a brief patrol of Skagerrak waters, from where she returned to Wilhelmshaven and passed through the Kiel Canal en route to Gdynia (which the Germans called Gotenhafen at the time) in order to divert the Allies' attention from the battleships *Scharnhorst* and *Gneisenau*, which were both moving in a westward direction. The *Deutschland* underwent an overhaul in the shipyard in Gdańsk (called Danzig by the Germans). Having completed dock trials, the ship was redesignated on January 25 at Hitler's personal request from a "Panzerschiff" to a heavy cruiser and at the same time renamed from *Deutschland* to *Lützow* (in honor of a baron von Lützow, a Prussian officer from the period of the Napoleonic Wars). The battleship's name was changed for three reasons: firstly, North-Atlantic operations being planned at the time required secrecy and concealment of German warships for as long as was possible; secondly, a heavy cruiser *Lützow* (of the *Admiral Hipper*-class) was being built and soon to be sold to the USSR, which was also worth camouflaging; thirdly and most importantly, in the event of sinking the ship, the enemy could possibly exploit such a fact for propaganda purposes by foretelling an end to Germany not unlike the end of the ship named after her.

Front view. Note the distinct underwater bulges on the hull.

Back view. Note that quarterdeck level is very low above the waterline.

In December the *Lützow* received communications about a forthcoming operation in the Atlantic Ocean. Resupplied with ammunition, the ship executed a range of drills in the Bay of Gdańsk from February 16 to 27. Accompanied by the cruiser *Emden* and the tanker *Nordmark*, on March 12 the *Lützow* departed for Swinemünde. The winter of 1940 was very harsh and the ship got covered in ice. As a result she had to be sent to Kiel on March 14 for a replacement of the propeller screws, which had been damaged by the ice.

When stationed at Wilhemshaven, the cruiser was assigned to Group 2 of Operation *Weserübung*, planned as an invasion of Denmark and Norway. Group 2 was tasked with seizing the city of Trondheim. One of the ship's engines malfunctioned at the last moment, though, and on April 7 the cruiser, reassigned to Group 5, arrived at Kiel. There she joined the other ships of her group: the heavy cruiser *Blücher*, the light cruiser *Emden*, torpedo boats and a flotilla of minesweepers. Group 5's mission was to take control of Oslofjord fortifications and to take over the Norwegian capital. Led by *Konteradmiral* Oskar Kummetz aboard the *Blücher*, the group departed on April 8. The warships were carrying 2,000 Wehrmacht mountain troops, over 400 of whom were aboard the *Lützow*.

As the German invasion of Norway was in progress, an unaware Vice Admiral Horton of Great Britain issued orders for several submarine flotillas to take positions in the Kattegat and the Skagerrak as well as along Norway's southwest coast for support of an intended British operation. At 1906 hours on April 8 the men on the *Blücher* sighted a torpedo launched at the Germans. The submarine boat *HMS Triton* deployed a total of ten torpedoes aimed at the group, with none of them reaching the target, though. At around 2325 the *Lützow's* radio service intercepted an order to switch off the coastal lights—a clear indication that the German attack would not be a surprise for the Norwegians. Shortly before midnight the *Blücher* passed the outer ring of Norwegian coastal batteries, with the *Lützow* and the cruiser *Emden* following right behind. The group entered the Oslofjord at a speed of 7 knots. At the break of dawn the speed was increased to 12 knots as the ships approached the narrowest section of the fjord, the Drøbak Sound, stretching several hundred meters across. Then, at around 0500 a.m., the Norwegians' searchlights illuminated the *Blücher*. The exposed cruiser was put under fire from the 28cm guns of the Oscarsborg Fortress, which was located nearby in the sound.

The subsequent exchange of fire over a distance of 1.8km resulted in the *Lützow* taking three hits from the 15cm guns of the

Norwegian Oscarsborg Kopås battery. The first shell had impacted the "A" turret of the main battery, leaving four of the ship's crewmen wounded. The second round had penetrated the deck. The ship's hospital rooms were damaged in the burst, which instantly killed two soldiers and wounded the ship's medic with six other soldiers. The third hit was on the crane, killing three seamen and injuring nine others. The heavy shelling forced the naval group to withdraw and exit the fjord. With fires already raging aboard the *Blücher*, she took two more hits from an underwater torpedo launcher. The crew attempted to steer into shallows, but a number of explosions throughout the warship caused her to capsize and sent her sinking with nearly a thousand seamen and soldiers onboard.

Having lost his flagship, Kummetz moved onto the *Lützow*. When the soldiers had been dropped off the ship at Sonsbukten, the *Lützow* and the *Emden* retreated to a naval base at Horten. The German air forces then mounted bombing raids on the coast. By the afternoon of April 9 most Norwegian fortresses had been taken. By 1900 hours the Germans had seized Drøbak. A day later they captured Kaholm with fire support from the *Lützow* and other ships. Norway announced capitulation shortly thereafter. The *Lützow*, the *Emden* and the torpedo boat *Möwe* could cast anchor at Oslo.

The damage inflicted on the cruiser forced the Kriegsmarine authorities to recall the *Lützow* for necessary repairs. The remaining part of Group 5 had remained in Norway. On her way back, while steaming at full speed at 0129 hours on April 11, the *Lützow* took a hit from a British submarine boat, the *HMS Spearfish*. The torpedo exploded at the stern of the warship, jamming the rudder and breaking off both propellers. A wide gap broke open along the hull, causing the risk of the entire stern falling off. The ship took in more than 1,300 tons of water as a result. She laid over on the starboard side with a considerable change of trim. Around 0400 the ship received assistance from submarine chasers and torpedo boats, which the *Lützow*'s crewmen were moved onto. The cruiser was subsequently towed back to Kiel, where she was docked at the Deutsche Werke shipyard on April 14. The invasion of Norway had cost the *Lützow* the lives of nineteen men, fifteen of whom were killed due to the torpedo attack. The cruiser's commander, August Thiele, was awarded the Knight's Cross of the Iron Cross for taking command of Group 5 during the Battle of Drøbak Sound.

The repairs, combined with a refitting of the *Lützow*, took almost one year. The warship was recommissioned into service on March 31, 1941. She returned to Norway in June with a destroyer escort as part of Operation *Sommerreise*. While en route, the group was sighted on June 13 by British reconnaissance aircraft. Following this, British torpedo bombers raided the ships during evening hours. The *Lützow* took a hit on the starboard side just aft of the funnel and very soon developed a list by 18 degrees. The machine room and electrical power plant had

The amidship area. The "Bruno" turret is trained to starboard.

been damaged and required emergency repairs, after which the cruiser had to return to Kiel. Even while undergoing thorough repairs in the shipyard, she had to repel several attacks mounted by British aircraft.

The *Lützow's* overhaul took until mid-January of 1942. On the 18th the cruiser departed Kiel and headed for Gdynia. Due to extensive ice cover in the Baltic Sea, a damaged propeller screw forced the crew to stop at Swinemünde. The sea conditions improved in April, allowing the ship to start naval drills. On May 10 the crew reported readiness for further action.

Combat activity from Norwegian bases

On May 12 the *Lützow* departed Swinemünde, setting a course for Bornholm. Three days later the ship followed the blockade runner *Sperrbrecher 13* with an escort of four destroyers headed for Kristiansand, Norway. Although an assault by submarines posed a very real threat and aerial reconnaissance traffic was all but constant, the group avoided detection by the British all the way to the destination, the Kravenesfjord off Kristiansand. The *Lützow* cast anchor there on May 17 at 0520 a.m.. Continuing their journey, the warships took a brief stop in the Grimstadfjord off Bergen, passed through Trondheim on May 19, and eventually made Bogen near Narvik five days later. The group joined the *Admiral Scheer*, which had been waiting at anchor there.

The Bogen-stationed warships formed Combat Group no. 2 (*Kampfgruppe 2*) as of June 4. *Konteradmiral* Kummetz chose the *Lützow* to be his flagship. From June 8 through 10 his task force practiced combat maneuvers in the Ofotfjord and the Vestjord. As an operation codenamed *Rösselsprung* was announced in early July (its objective was to destroy the Allied convoy PQ 17 on its way to Arkhangelsk with supplies for the USSR), the *Lützow* and the *Admiral Scheer* left Bogen on the 2nd with an escort of the destroyers *Z 24*, *Z 27*, *Z 28*, *Z 29* and *Z 30* to rendezvous with the German battleship *Tirpitz*. An unexpected shallow appeared in the *Lützow's* way at 0242 on July 2 in Tjeldsund. The ship's hull was damaged in the process and the water found its way inside. The hull's outer layer had been affected over a length of 70–80m. *Konteradmiral* Kummetz's flag was transferred to the *Admiral Scheer*, as the *Lützow's* crew was forced to take the damaged ship back to Bogen. From there she cruised through the Lofjord near Trondheim and arrived at Swinemünde on July 12. With fuel and ammunition removed from the ship, she was docked on July 13 for repairs at the Deutsche Werke shipyard in Kiel.

A number of small incidents took place during the overhaul. On September 23 a fire broke out in the shipyard. Four days later fire was set by accident in an ammunition magazine. Still later, on November 4, the ship's "B" turret collided against a floating crane on undocking. The period of repairs at the shipyard provided an opportunity to make replacements for a considerable part of the crew. The overhaul had been completed by October 30, 1942. Soon thereafter, on November 9, assisted by the destroyers *ZH 1* and *Karl Galster*, the *Lützow* was able to set out into the Baltic Sea for combat drills off Cape Arkona. In early December the warship took part in group maneuvers in the Bay of Gdańsk and central Baltic waters. On December 8 the cruiser joined the destroyers *Karl Galster*, *Theodor Riedel* and *Z 31* to leave Gdynia on a cruise to Norway. The group reached Bogen without incident on December 12, 1942. Two of the destroyers, the *Z 31* and the *Theodor Riedel*, accompanied the cruiser farther to the Altafjord on the night of December 17. This Far North destination was an anchorage for a naval force that included the *Admiral Hipper*, the light cruisers *Nürnberg* and *Köln*, and some smaller vessels. When the *Lützow* arrived, the group was left by the *Admiral Scheer*.

The *Lützow* left the fjord on December 30 together with the other heavy cruiser, *Admiral Hipper*, and the 5th Flotilla destroyers in order to carry out Operation *Rogenbogen*. The warships cruised along the Norwegian coastline at first until they headed out to the open sea. Their target was the JW-51B convoy, comprising fourteen Allied ships which had set out from Loch Ewe on December 22. However, the commander of the German task force, *Konteradmiral* Kummetz, had not been informed about the strength of the convoy's escort. Confronted by a storm, the British ships had separated and the JW-51B group eventually consisted of nine vessels escorted by the destroyers *HMS Onslow*, *Oribi*, *Obedient*, *Obdurate*, *Orwell* and *Achates* along with several smaller warships. Additional protection was being provided by the light cruisers *HMS Sheffield* and *Jamaica*, the destroyer *Opportune*, and later on also by the *Matchless*. At a longer distance from the convoy were the battleship *HMS Anson*, the heavy cruiser *Cumberland* and three destroyers. Lastly, the British had positioned a number of submarines along the way to the Altafjord to patrol the area.

The weather at sea was very unfavorable on December 31. *Konteradmiral* Kummetz dispersed the German force in order to find the location of the convoy. At around 0820 hours the escort of the Allied convoy spotted the German destroyers on a course at a right angle to theirs. One hour later the Germans opened fire upon the *Obdurate* and the *Achates*. The destroyers *Onslow* and *Orwell* responded with an attack on the *Admiral Hipper*, chasing the German cruiser away for a period of time. The latter was able to return after nearly an hour. Her fire then caused severe damage to the *Onslow*, and continued with an attack on the *Orwell*. Twenty minutes later the German ships managed to sink a minesweeper. The *Admiral Hipper* opened fire on other convoy ships but failed to score any hits except for some that reached and inflicted damage on the destroyers *Achates* and *Obedient*. At the same time the *Lützow* passed next to the British convoy, failing to notice it because of the very poor visibility. In consequence of uninterrupted attacks on the *Admiral Hipper*, the ship had been hit three times by the light cruisers. The explosions resulted in heavy losses to the crew and damage to the engine room, which caused the ship's speed to drop to 15 knots. This made Kummetz decide to withdraw his force to the west. Fifteen minutes before midday the *Lützow* eventually opened fire on the convoy, which was now being defended by the damaged *Onslow*. The other British ships had laid smoke screens and mounted another attack. Adhering to the commander's orders, the *Lützow* would not take "unnecessary risks"; the cruiser broke off the assault and turned to the west in order to catch up with the rest of the group. The unsuccessful operation had left the Germans with a sunken destroyer *Friedrich Eckoldt* and her entire crew lost with the ship. The *Lützow* and the five surviving destroyers returned to the Altafjord unharmed. On the British side the losses had amounted to the destroyer *Achates* and the single minesweeper. Three other destroyers had suffered some damage from the *Admiral Hipper*. This engagement, later to be known as the Battle of the Barents Sea, had turned out to be a German fiasco, since not one of the convoy ships had been sunk.

The German group returned into the Norwegian fjords on January 1, 1943. The ships cast anchor at various locations between Bogen and the Kåfjorden in order to mislead the Allies' aerial reconnaissance. In March, when the battleships *Tirpitz* and *Scharnhorst* came to Bogen, the *Lützow* was moved into the Kåfjorden near Alta, where group maneuvers were being drilled. An operation codenamed *Husar* and planned for the summer of 1943 (in which the *Lützow* was to be fighting Soviet shipping in the Kara Sea) could not materialize because of recurring engine troubles. After one of these malfunctions on July 14, the ship was scheduled to return to her native shipyard in Germany, for which she set out on September 23. The journey was made in stages: the cruiser and her escort took a stop in the Skjomen fjord; on the 26th the ships passed the Arctic Circle. As the group was en route, advancing southwards, it was harassed with unsuccessful attacks attempted by American and British shipboard air forces. Eventually, the *Lützow* and the escorting destroyers *Paul Jacobi*, *Erich Steinbrinck* and *Z 38* reached Kiel on September 29, 1943. Ultimately, the cruiser anchored at Gdynia two days later, on October 1, where actual repair work began, to be continued later on at Libau[3]. When USAAF bombers raided Gdynia on October 9, as the maintenance was in progress, the cruiser was fortunate to avoid damage in the process.

Equipped with new supplies, the *Lützow* went through dock trials between February and March of 1944; later, when stationed at Libau, the cruiser proceeded with sea trials. Starting in mid-March, the cruiser participated in intensive training maneuvers. These were performed together with the cruisers *Prinz Eugen*, *Admiral Scheer*, *Nürnberg* and

Starboard bow view.

General characteristics (July 1942)

Displacement	Design: 12,630 tons Full load: 14,290 tons
Length	187.9 meters
Beam	20.69 meters
Draft	At design displacement: 5.78 meters At full-load displacement: 7.25 meters
Propulsion	Eight MAN nine-cylinder Diesel engines rated at 48,390 horsepower
Top speed	28 knots
Range	17,400 nautical miles at 13 knots
Armament	6 x 28 cm L/52 SK C/28 (2 x III) 8 x 15 cm L/55 SK C/28 (8 x I) 6 x 10.5 cm L/65 C/33 (3 x II) 8 x 3.7 cm L/83 C/30 (4 x II) 29 x 2 cm L/65 C/38 (5 x IV, 9 x I) 8 x 53.3 cm torpedo tubes (2 x IV)
Armor	Main belt: 80mm decreasing to 50mm at the bottom Decks: upper 18mm; main 30-45 mm Main battery turrets: fore 140 mm, side 75-80 mm, aft 170 mm, roof 50-105 mm Barbettes: 125 mm Secondary battery: 10 mm Conning tower: 50-150 mm
Radar equipment	FuMO 22 radar (antenna on main rangefinder) FuMB 4 *Samos* passive radar detector with FuMB Ant 7 *Timor* antenna (on main rangefinder) and four FuMB Ant 4 *Sumatra* antennas (below main rangefinder)
Complement	Around 1,100 officers and enlisted men

Emden, with support from torpedo boats, submarines and submarine chasers. For June the *Lützow* relocated to the Finnish coast, where she practiced combat drills with the *Prinz Eugen* and torpedo boats. The warship was stationed back in Gdynia from July 8, 1944, and while there, the *Lützow* took part in a fleet parade to welcome the Chief of Fleet, *Generaladmiral* Schniewind, who was visiting the base. The admiral made his inspection of the fleet from the cruiser *Nürnberg*, reviewing virtually all the large warships still in service with the Kriegsmarine: *Prinz Eugen*, *Lützow*, *Admiral Scheer*, *Admiral Hipper* as well as *Köln*, *Leipzig* and *Emden*. Only the *Tirpitz* was missing, staying immobilized in a Norwegian fjord at the time.

In late July the *Lützow* became part of a task force named *Kampfgruppe 2*. This unit also included the *Prinz Eugen* and the 6th Destroyer Flotilla. Their primary task was protection and delivery of supplies to Wehrmacht forces engaged in fighting in Latvia and Estonia. From September 22 through 25 of 1944, after Finland had terminated its alliance with Germany, the *Lützow* was involved in escorting convoys which transported German ground troops that were retreating from the north. In October and November the cruiser was raiding Red Army units in Klaipėda and on the Sworbe Peninsula[4]. Ammunition and fuel for the *Lützow* during this operation were supplied in Gdynia. On December 18 the port became the target of a heavy air raid mounted by RAF bombers. The *Lützow* was fortunate again, as she did not sustain any damage. The ship was moved to Pillau[5] towards the end of the month.

In early February of 1945 the cruisers *Lützow*, *Admiral Scheer* and *Prinz Eugen* were deployed to East Prussia for bombardment operations against Soviet military positions near Frauenburg[6] and Elbing[7]. In the second half of March the ship was active in a defense of Gdynia, Kępa Oksywska and Hel from the progress of the Soviet army. She was also fighting off air raids at the same time. The fighting in the bay continued into early April. The *Lützow* sustained light damage caused by Soviet artillery fire on the 4th. On April 8 the Soviets sunk a German supply ship, the *Franken*. In consequence, both the *Lützow* and the *Prinz Eugen* were forced to leave the combat theater and cruise to Swinemünde.

On April 16, as the *Lützow* was stationed in the Kaiserfahrt[8], the RAF's No. 617 Squadron mounted an attack. One of the Tallboy bombs (with a weight exceeding 5 tons) deployed from the British Lancasters

Port quarter view.

blew up thirty meters from the ship. The hull was severely damaged and the cruiser listed by 56 degrees. Two other bombs of 500kg each hit the aft storage of 28cm rounds at the stern—these, however, failed to explode, fortunately for the ship.

On the next day *Konteradmiral* Thiele came aboard the *Lützow*. While visiting, he wanted to make sure that the cruiser's batteries were functional enough to allow her use in defense of Swinemünde, as the port was of great importance for the Germans: it was the central rescue station for hundreds of thousands of refugees and wounded. After the cruiser's tilt was undone by resue ships and power restored at the main battery "A" turret, the *Lützow* was able to open fire on advancing front units of the Red Army. More and more crewmen were leaving the ship, with only those remaining who were needed to manage the turret, the battery operation instruments and the power supply. The anti-aircraft armament was dismantled and removed onto destroyers. The shelling of the Soviet army continued until May 3. With most of the ammunition depleted and no prospects of the situation improving, the Germans decided to blow up the ship in order to prevent her from being taken over by the Soviets. On May 4 a number of scuttling charges were detonated aboard the *Lützow*, sending the cruiser to the bottom.

Between the months of May and June the wreck of the *Lützow* was being investigated by Soviet committees, who were to determine the ship's future fate. A decision was reached in July of 1945 that the wreck would be raised from the bottom and towed to the USSR. Two years later the hull was successfully lifted. This provided an opportunity to search through the wreck. The "B" turret ammunition chamber turned out to contain approximately 300 rounds and propellant charges for the 28cm guns. There was also ammunition for 15cm guns, 10.5cm guns and 4cm guns aboard the ship. In June of 1947 the Soviets decided to scuttle the cruiser. To achieve that, bombs that ranged from 100kg to 1000kg were rigged at various points on the ship. On July 20 five towing boats were used to relocate the *Lützow* to Swinemünde, from where she was towed to the location of her planned sinking (near Kołobrzeg). The destination was reached on July 22 at 0825. The depth of the water in the area was approximately 110 meters. The whole spectacle was to be recorded on camera from aboard a chaser. The first explosion was heard two hours later—at 1025 the remotely detonated bomb damaged the conning tower and the rangefinder. The other two 100kg bombs failed to detonate. A second explosion was initiated at 1245. The 500kg bomb caused a fire onboard, but the cruiser was still afloat on the surface of the sea. The impatience of the Russian commander made him combine the third and fourth scheduled charges and blow up 1.5 tons of explosives in a single detonation. This final burst went off at 1545 as planned, covering the ship in smoke for three or four minutes. The cruiser reappeared, still floating. It was only at 1615 that she slowly began to go down. Shortly afterwards, the *Lützow* disappeared from view below the surface.

Literature

Deutschland/Lützow & Admiral Scheer & Admiral Graf Spee. http://deutschland-class.dk.

Waldemar Danielewicz, Mirosław Skwiot: *Pancerniki kieszonkowe cz. I, Deutschland / Lützow*. AJ-Press, 1997.

Waldemar Danielewicz, Tadeusz Skwiot: *Pancerniki kieszonkowe cz. 3, Deutschland / Lützow, Admiral Graf Spee, Admiral Scheer*. AJ-Press, 1999.

Endnotes

[1] Polish: Świnoujście
[2] Lithuanian: Klaipėda
[3] Latvian: Liepāja
[4] Estonian: Sõrve
[5] Russian: Baltiysk
[6] Polish: Frombork
[7] Polish: Elbląg
[8] Polish: Kanał Piastowski

Starboard side views of the hull and superstructures. All illustrations in this publication depict the *Lützow* as she looked during Operation *Rösselsprung* in July of 1942.

T3 DH

T3 DH

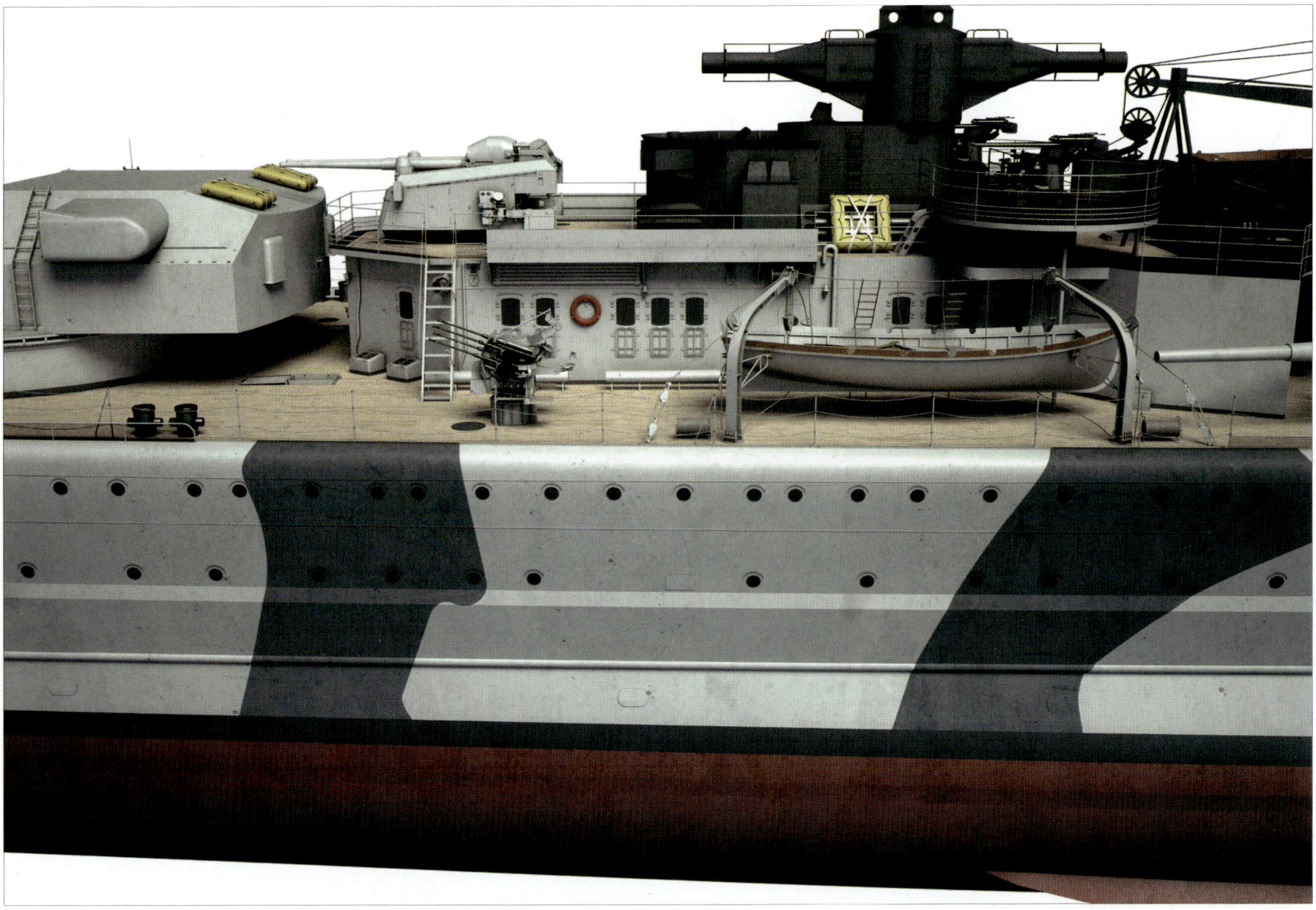

Port side views of the hull and superstructures.

DH

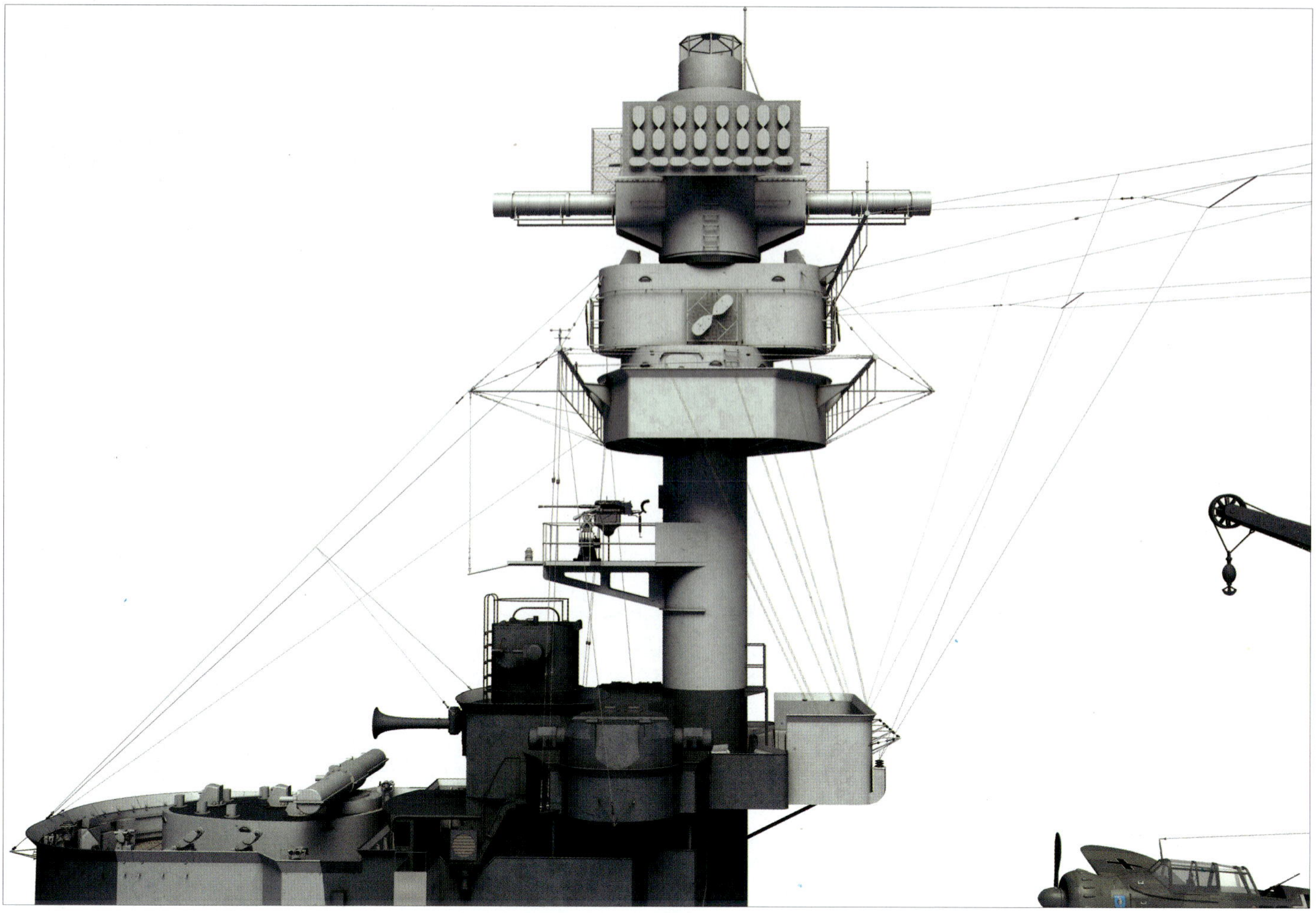

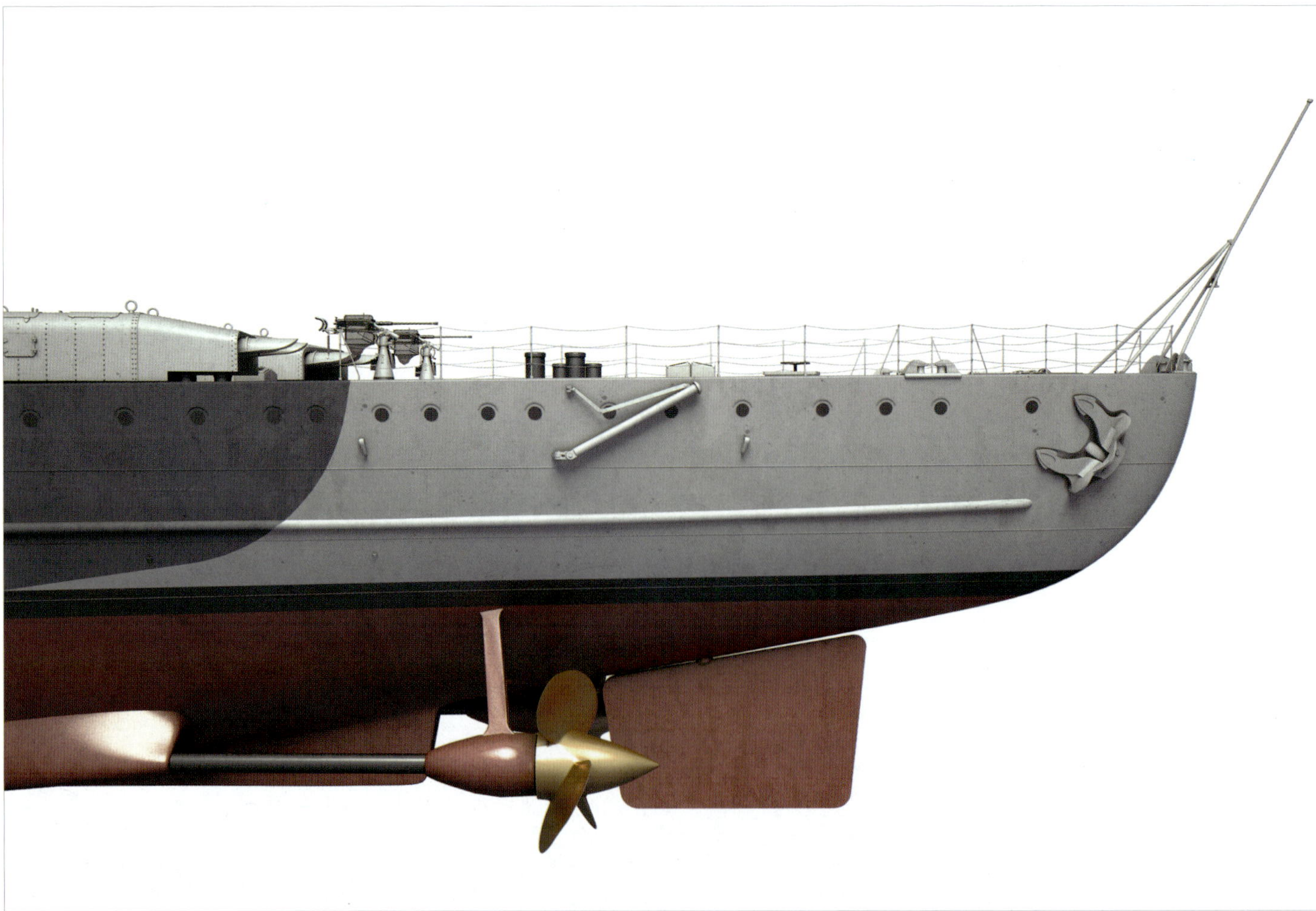

Top views of the decks and superstructures.

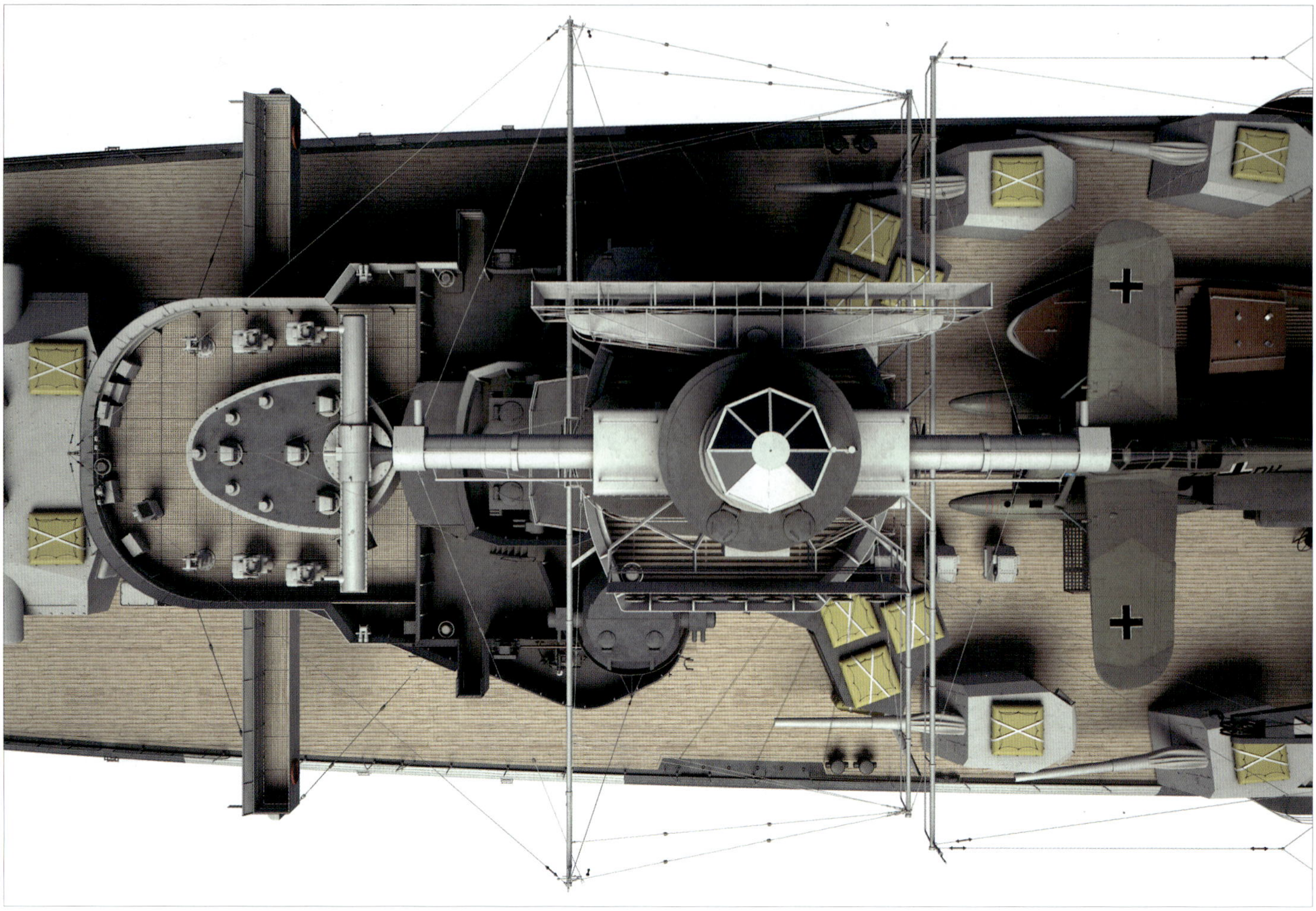

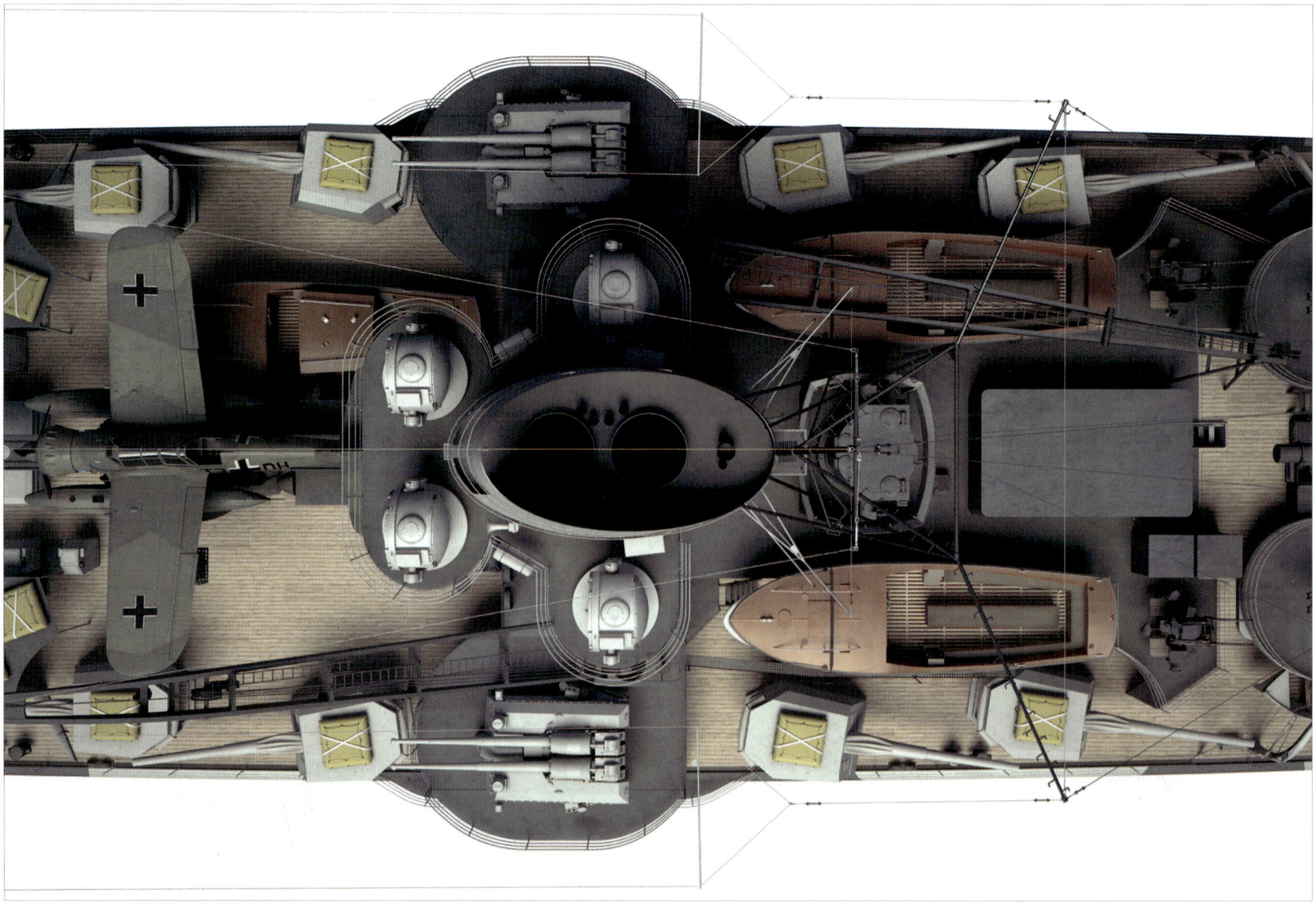

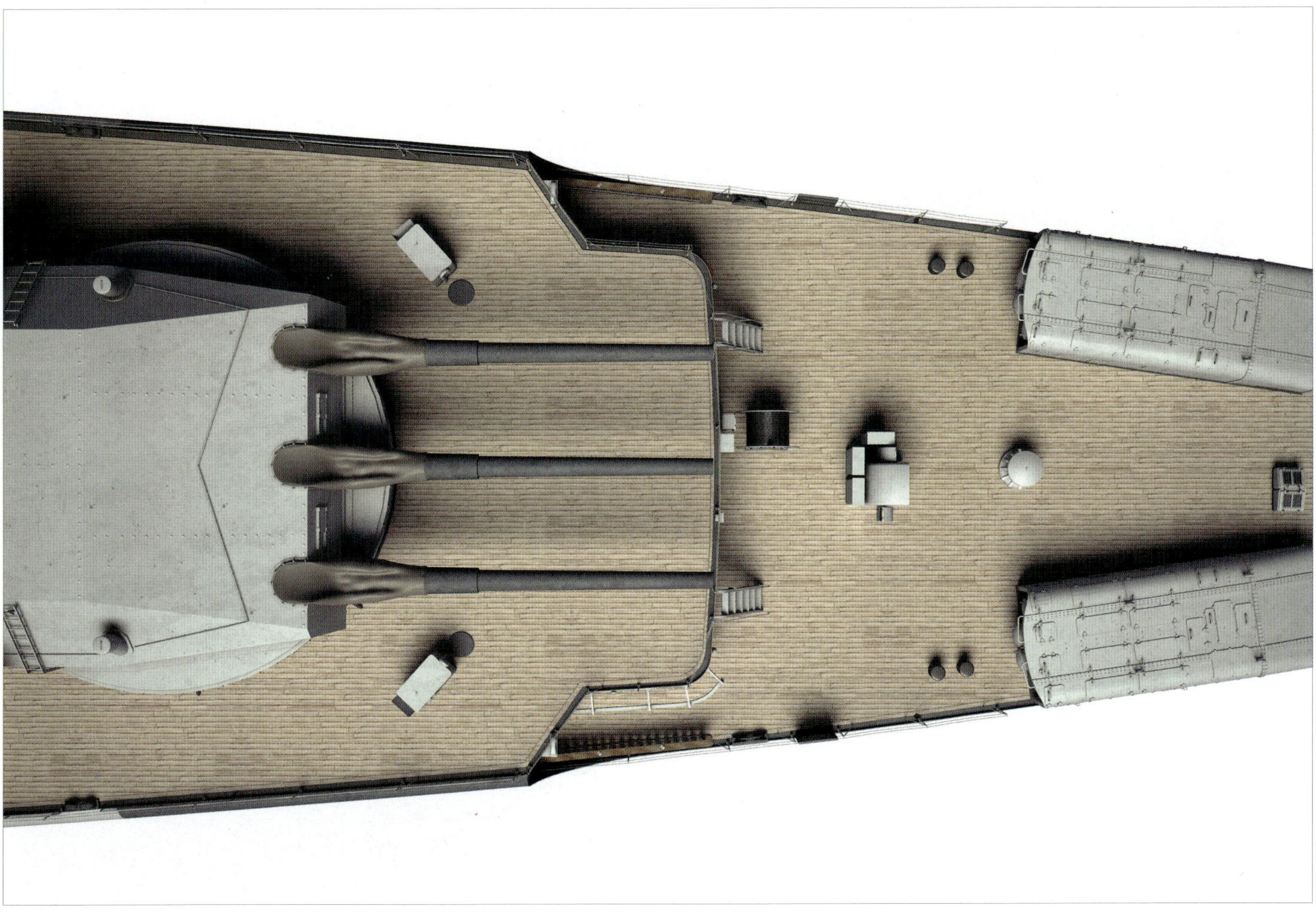

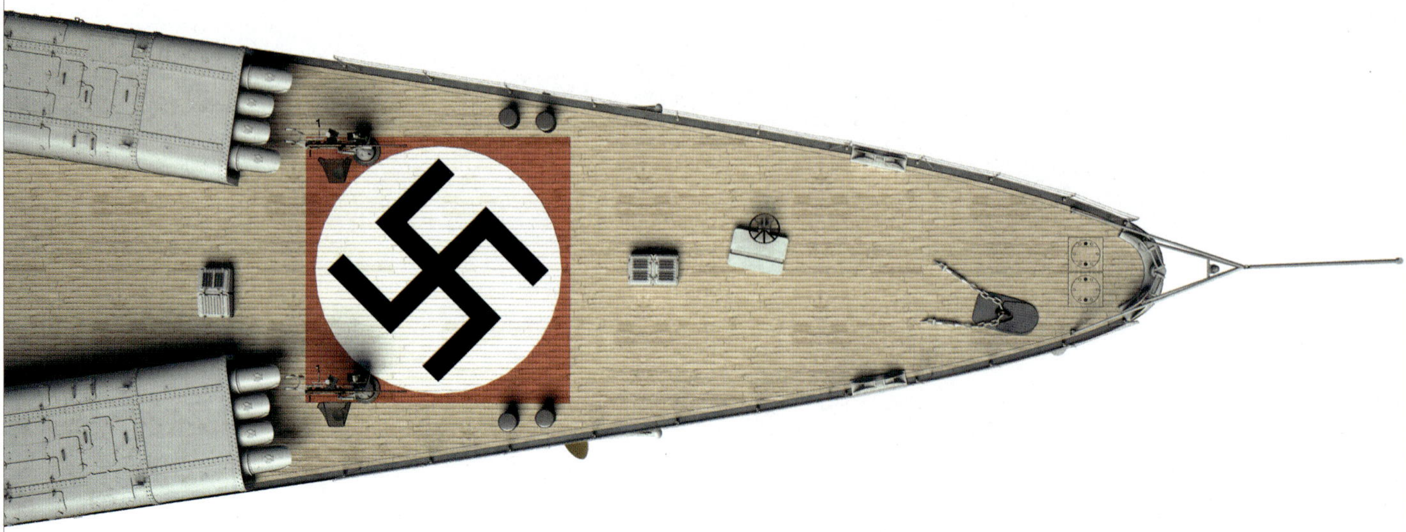

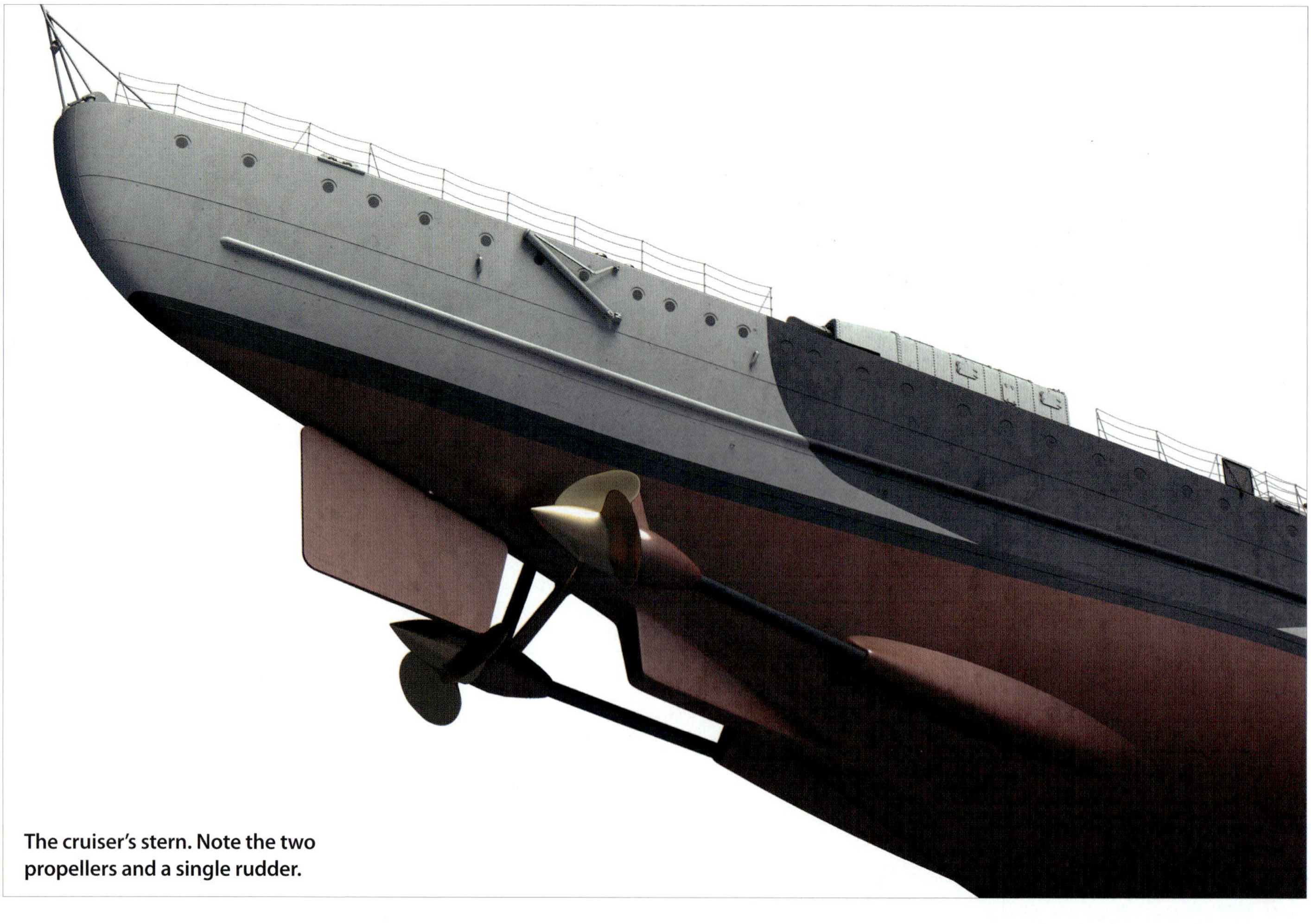

The cruiser's stern. Note the two propellers and a single rudder.

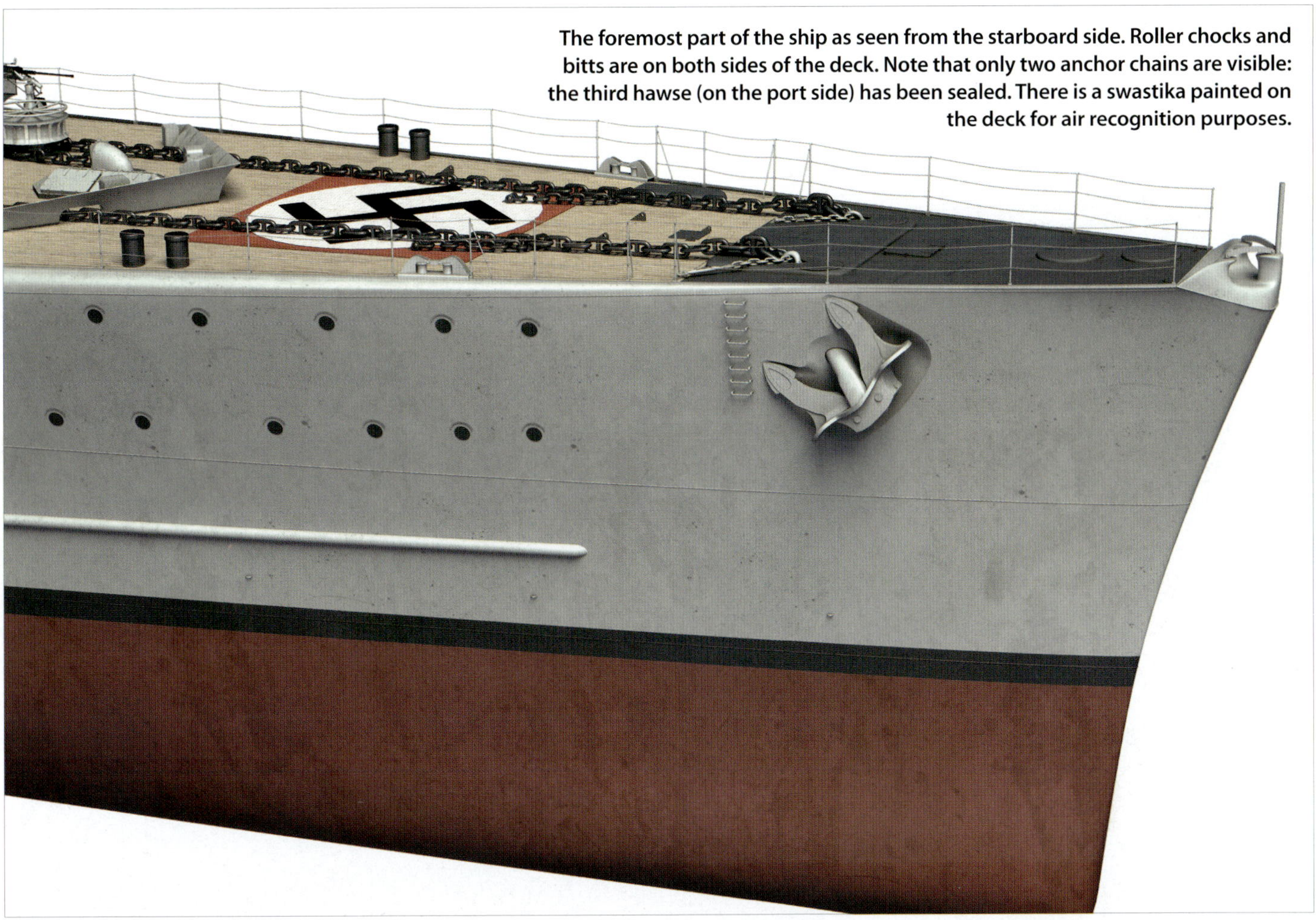

The foremost part of the ship as seen from the starboard side. Roller chocks and bitts are on both sides of the deck. Note that only two anchor chains are visible: the third hawse (on the port side) has been sealed. There is a swastika painted on the deck for air recognition purposes.

More views of the bow. This area was rebuilt in 1940 to create the so-called "Atlantic stem", which ensured better hull behavior at high seas. Also the bow crests have been erased and the rear port side anchor hawse has been sealed. Note the presence of the degaussing cable coming out of the hull on both sides of the ship.

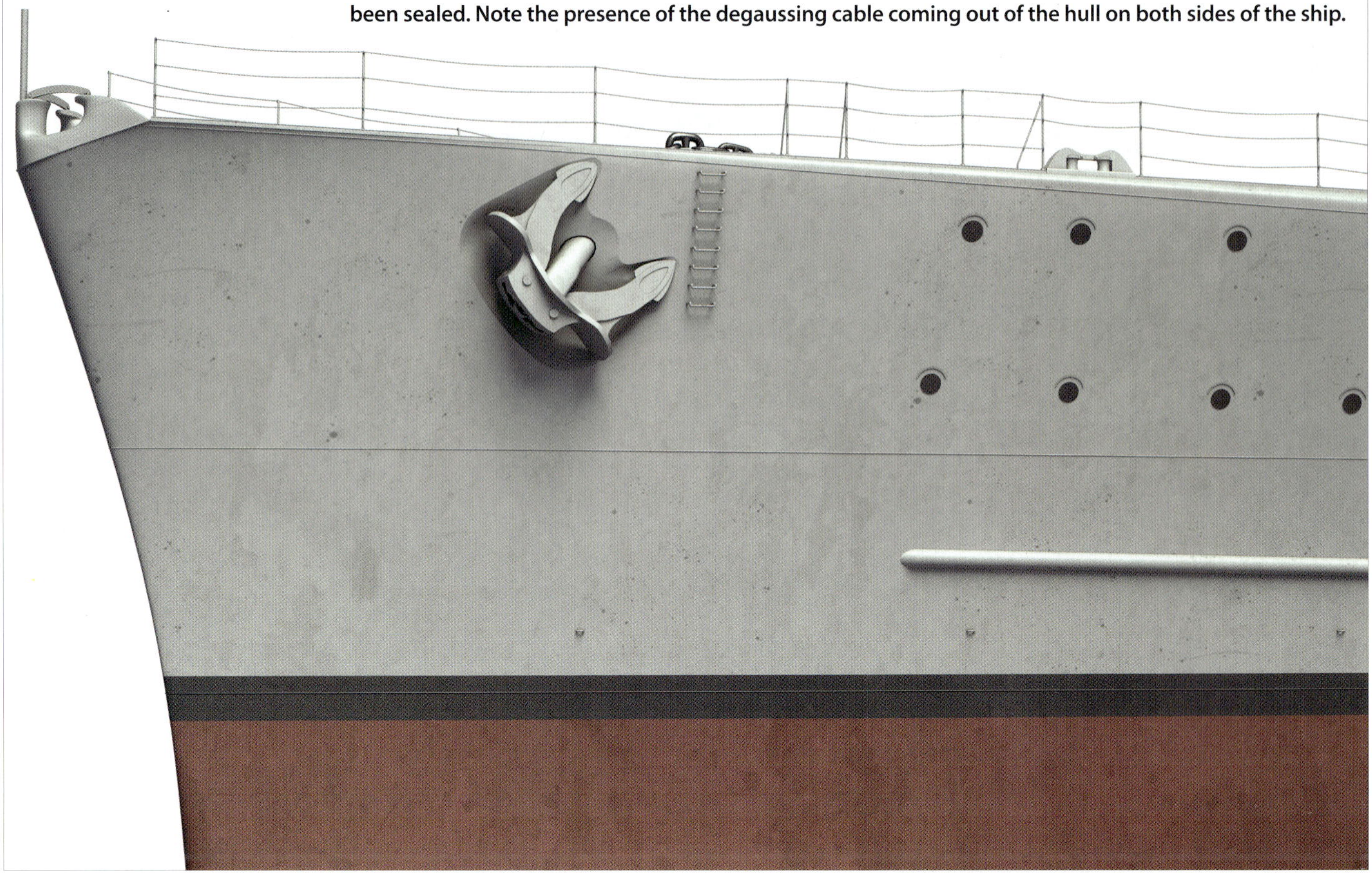

The forecastle deck. Note that the anchor chains are equipped with stoppers. The bow breakwater was installed during pre-war service as a result of experiences in heavy weather. Capstans can be seen just behind.

One of the foremost 2cm L/65 C/38 anti-aircraft guns on a single mount. This type replaced the very similar earlier C/30 gun. In 1942 there were nine such mounts installed on board.

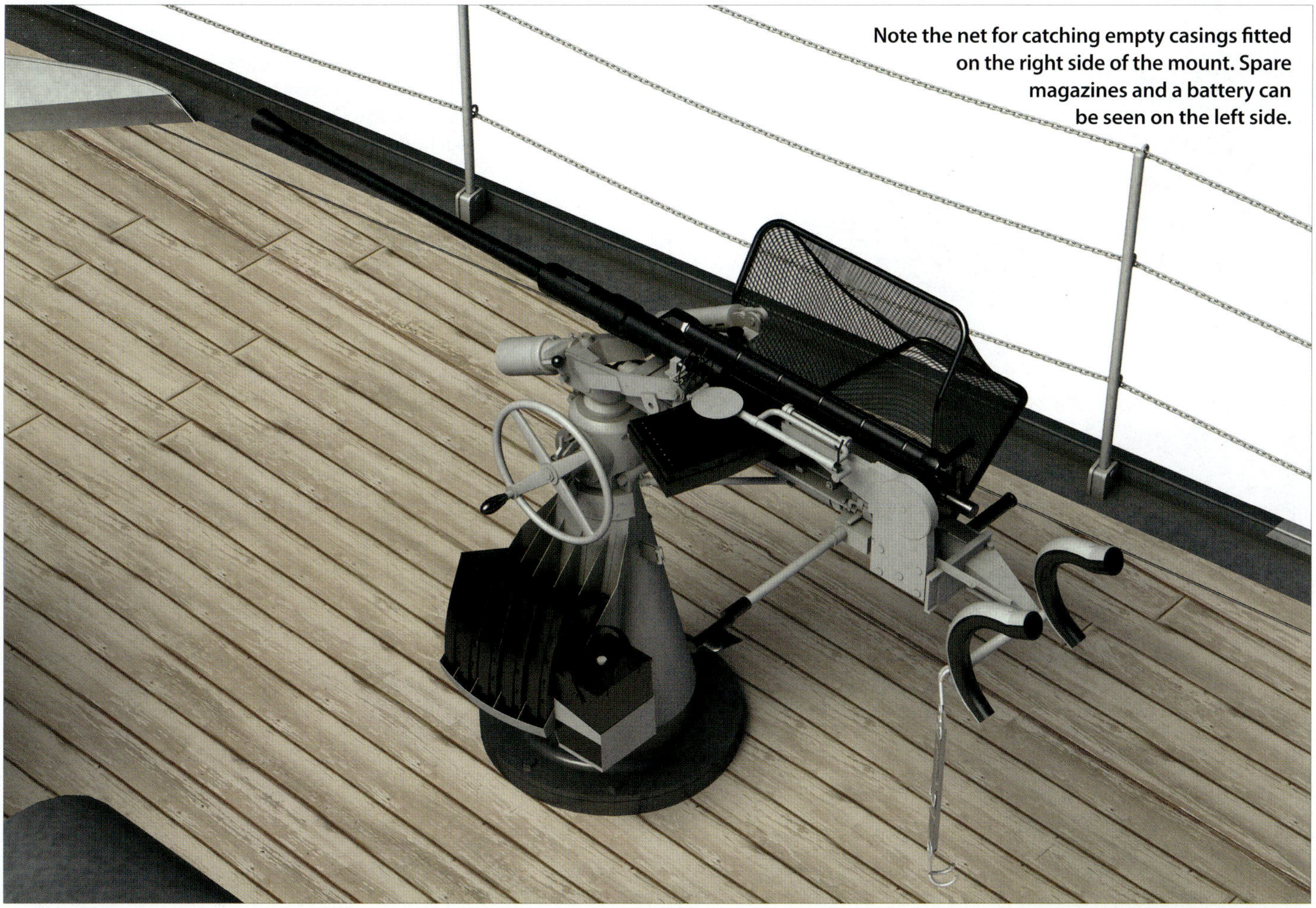

Note the net for catching empty casings fitted on the right side of the mount. Spare magazines and a battery can be seen on the left side.

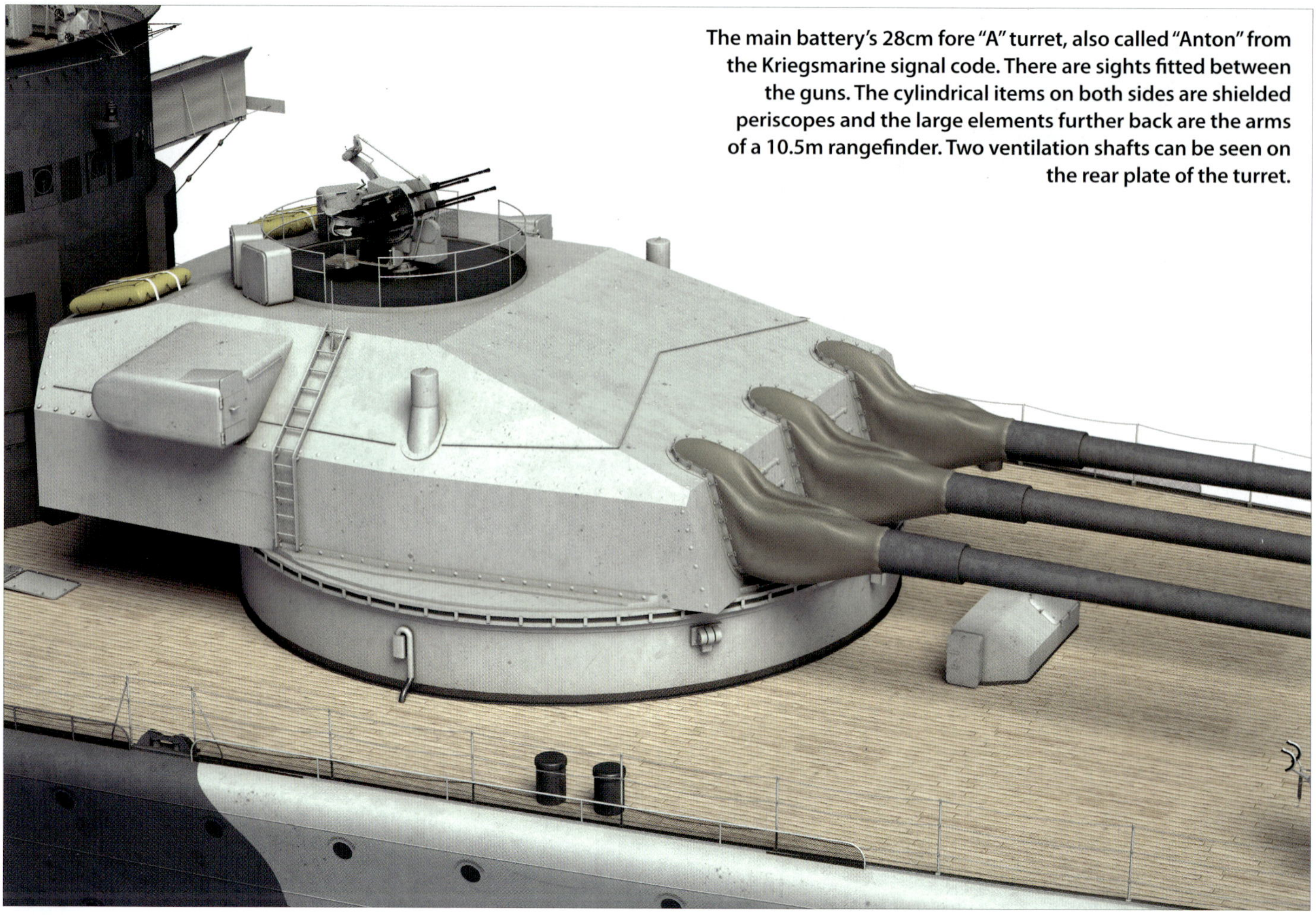

The main battery's 28cm fore "A" turret, also called "Anton" from the Kriegsmarine signal code. There are sights fitted between the guns. The cylindrical items on both sides are shielded periscopes and the large elements further back are the arms of a 10.5m rangefinder. Two ventilation shafts can be seen on the rear plate of the turret.

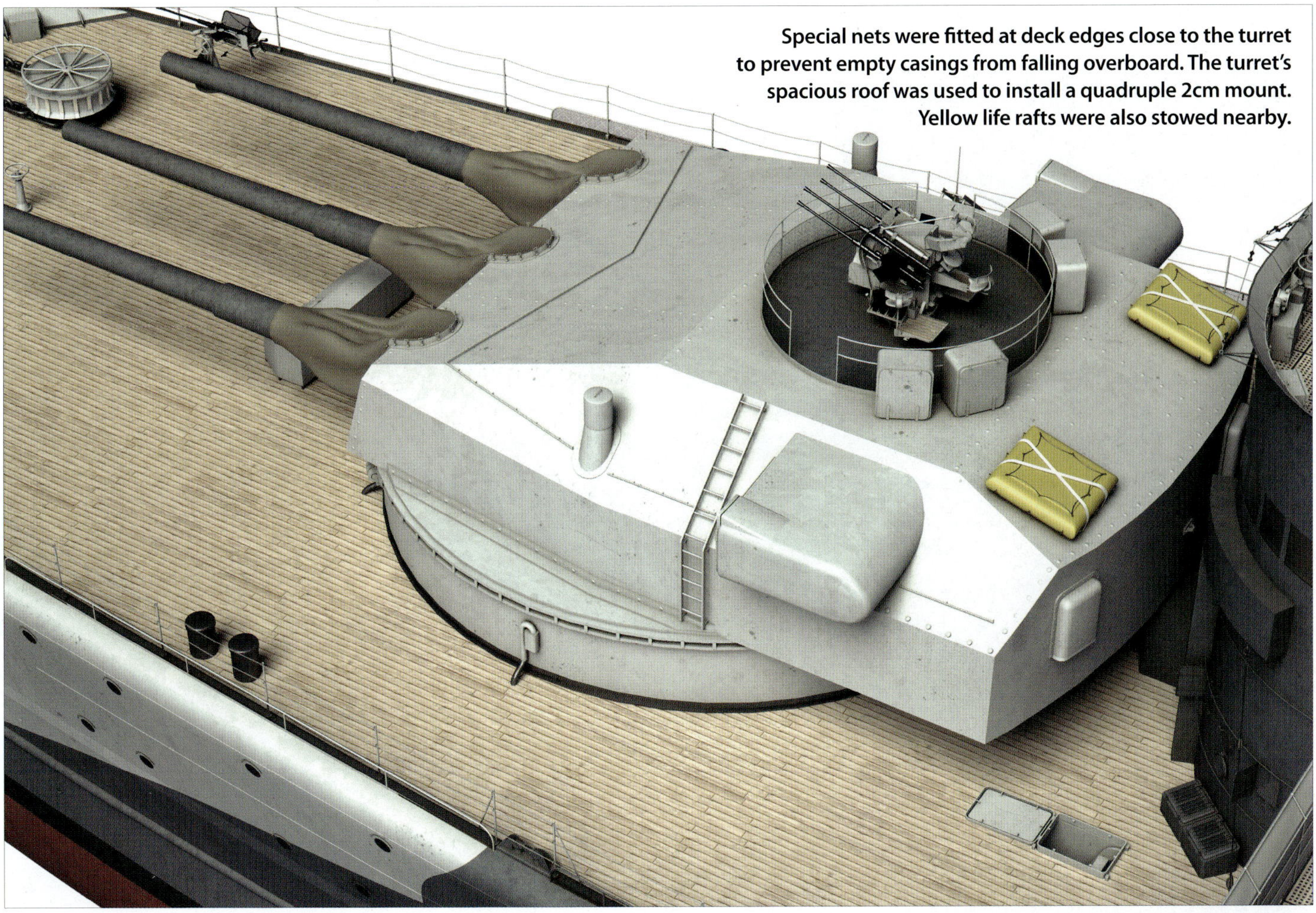

Special nets were fitted at deck edges close to the turret to prevent empty casings from falling overboard. The turret's spacious roof was used to install a quadruple 2cm mount. Yellow life rafts were also stowed nearby.

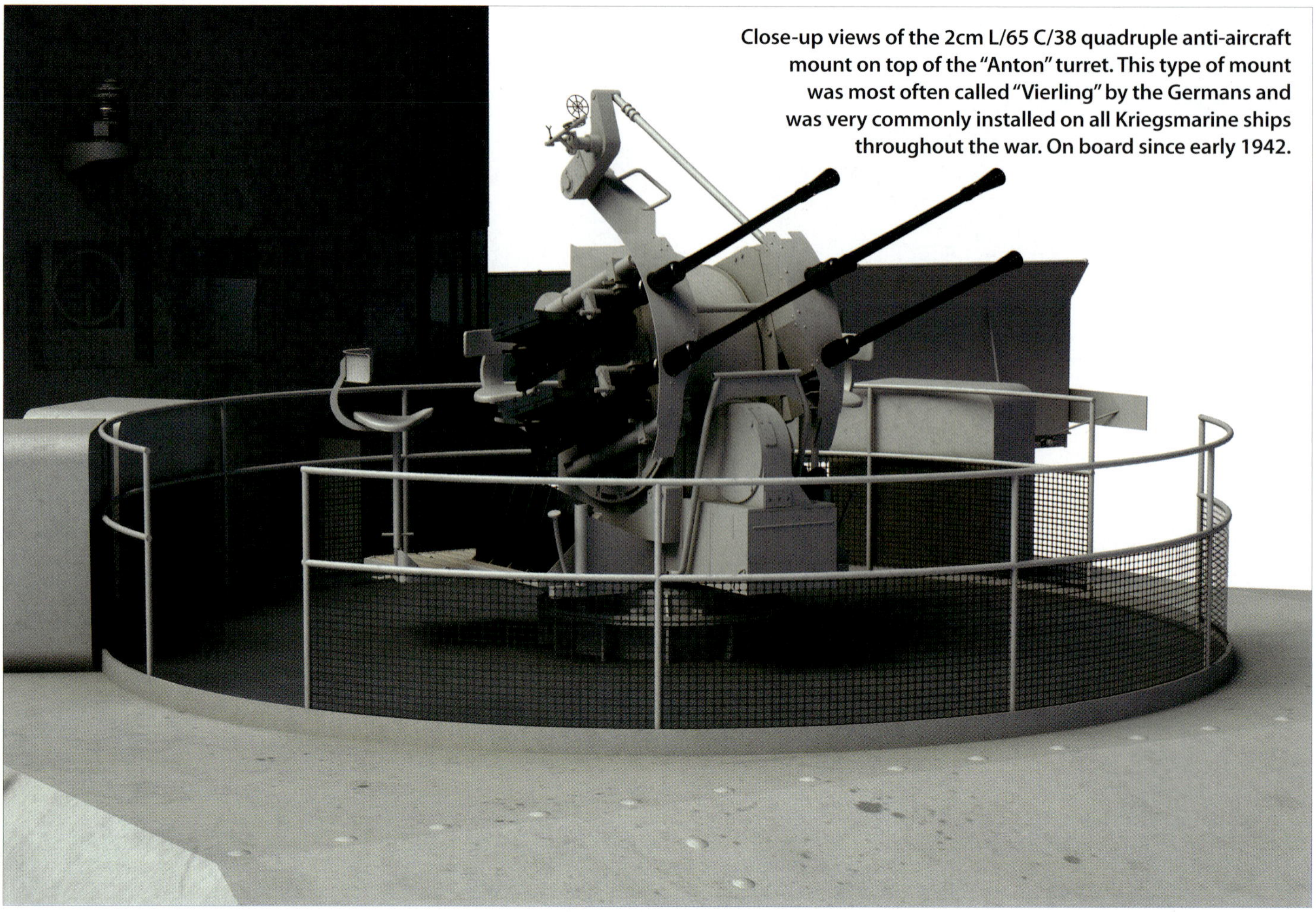

Close-up views of the 2cm L/65 C/38 quadruple anti-aircraft mount on top of the "Anton" turret. This type of mount was most often called "Vierling" by the Germans and was very commonly installed on all Kriegsmarine ships throughout the war. On board since early 1942.

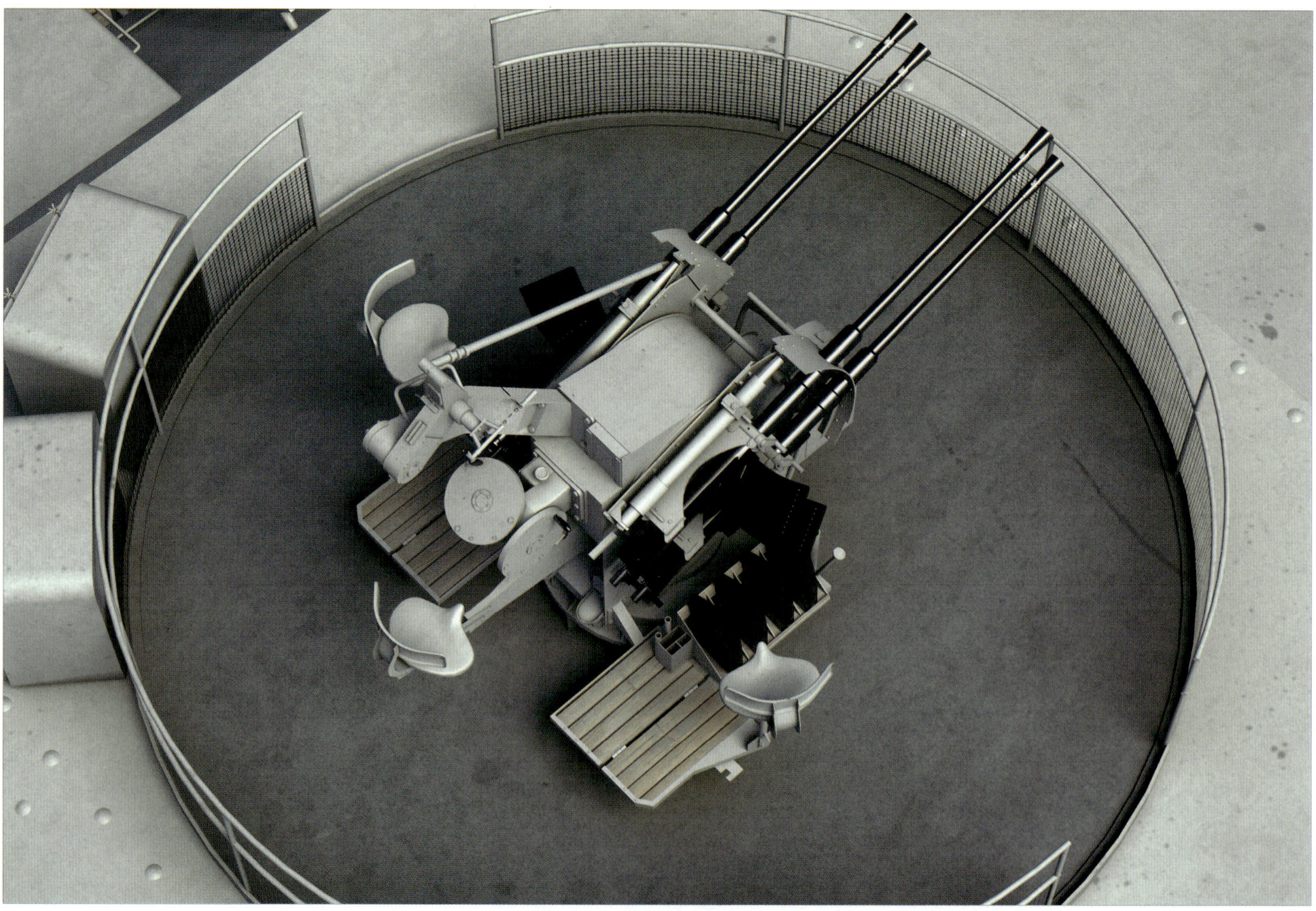

The seat at the back of the mount was for the gunner, whereas the side seats were for magazine loaders. Spare ammunition lockers can be seen near the railings.

The bottom part of the fore superstructure. Boat booms have been removed from the hull sides earlier on in the war, with only ladders and fittings left. A pair of single 2cm mounts is on each side of the superstructure.

A paravane stowed on the fore superstructure's side. The cylindrical containers on the deck are for barrel-cleaning equipment. There is one such container for each 28cm barrel.

A folding bridge on the starboard side. Note that it has a canvas cover around it. A lifebuoy and a position light can also be seen.

The rear bottom part of the fore superstructure. A twin 3.7cm anti-aircraft mount is installed on a platform on each side. Note the loudspeakers fitted to the platforms' shields. Life rafts are stowed on the roofs of crew shelters.

The open bridge on the fore superstructure. A compass repeater and several lockers can be seen at the front. The armored conning tower is in the center, with periscopes, sights and a large 7m rangefinder on its roof.

Optical equipment on the bridge: searchlight director (left) and target giver (right).

The rangefinder's left arm and a pair of binoculars at the wing of the bridge.

The middle part of the fore superstructure. Shielded 3m rangefinders can be seen on each side. A stabilized SL-2 heavy anti-aircraft artillery director is located on the center line with a siren fitted to its front shield.

Close-ups of a signal light on one of the superstructure decks.
A compass repeater can be seen nearby.

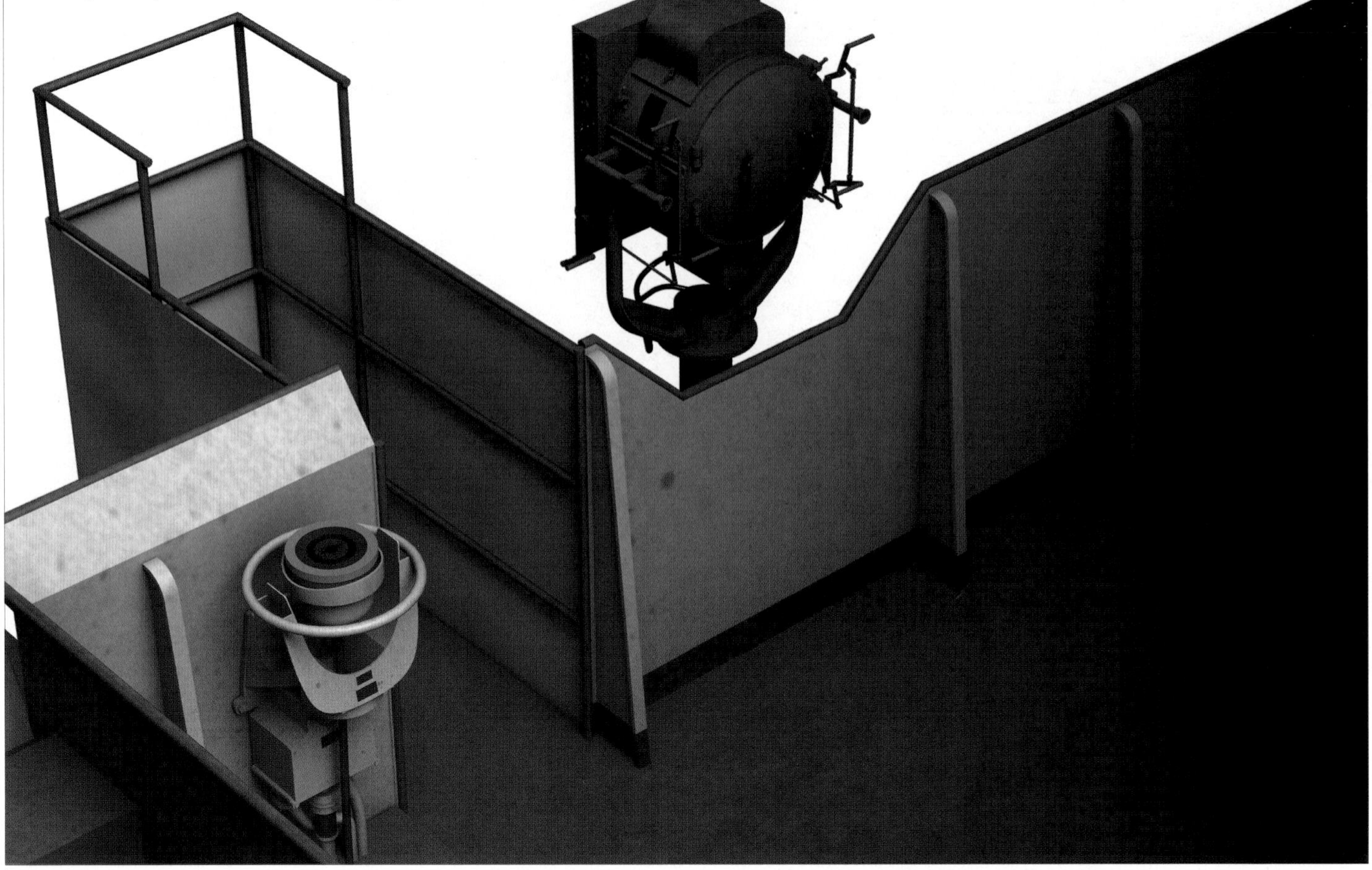

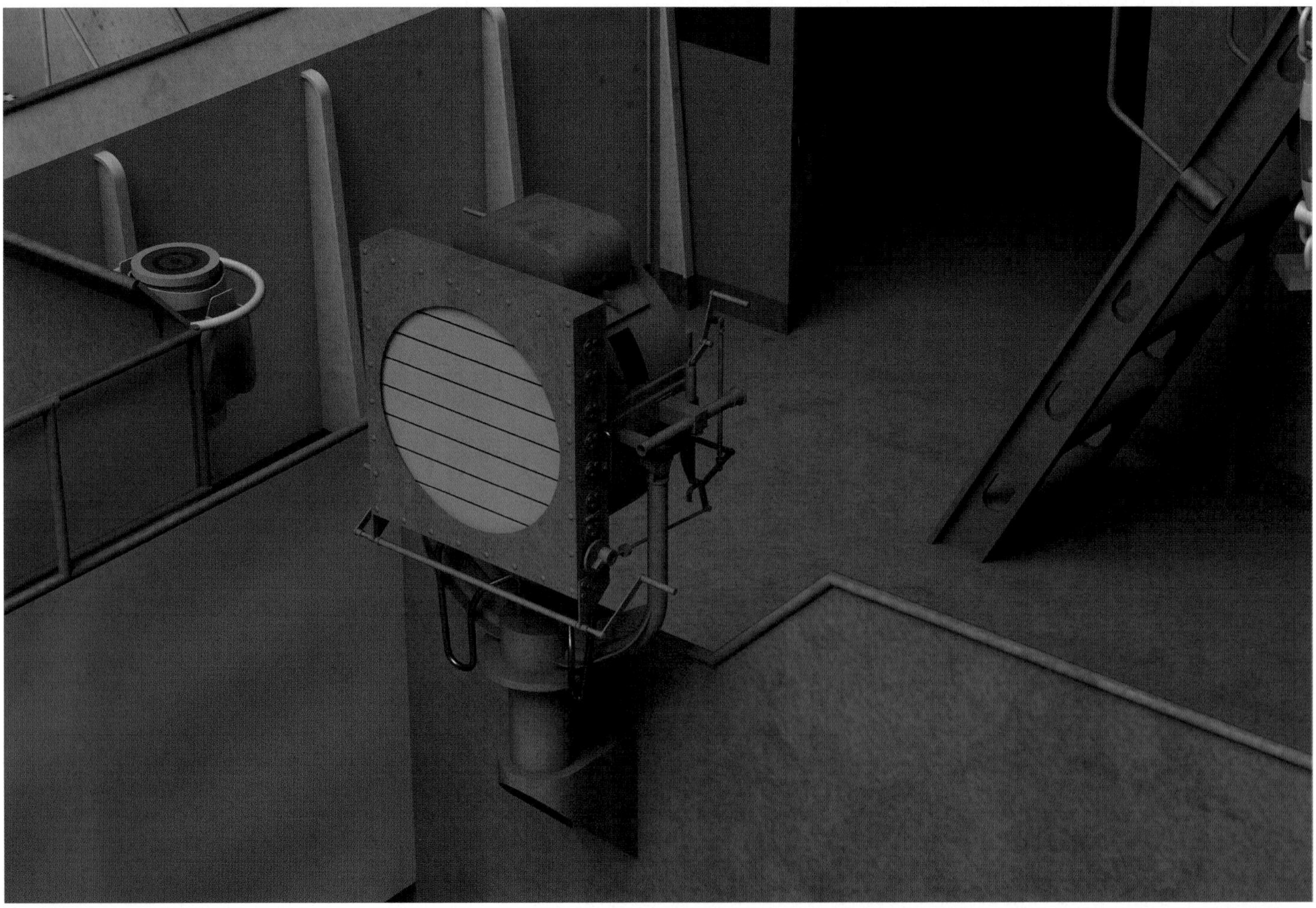

The flag platform at the rear of the superstructure is where the ship's signal flags were stowed, hanging under protective canvas sheets. Note also the antenna outriggers fitted to the rear shield.

A port side view of the 3m rangefinder and the SL-2 director.

The fore superstructure's searchlight platform. Early in the war a single 2cm mount was installed here. However, it suffered from poor firing angles and probably because of this it was later again replaced with a searchlight.

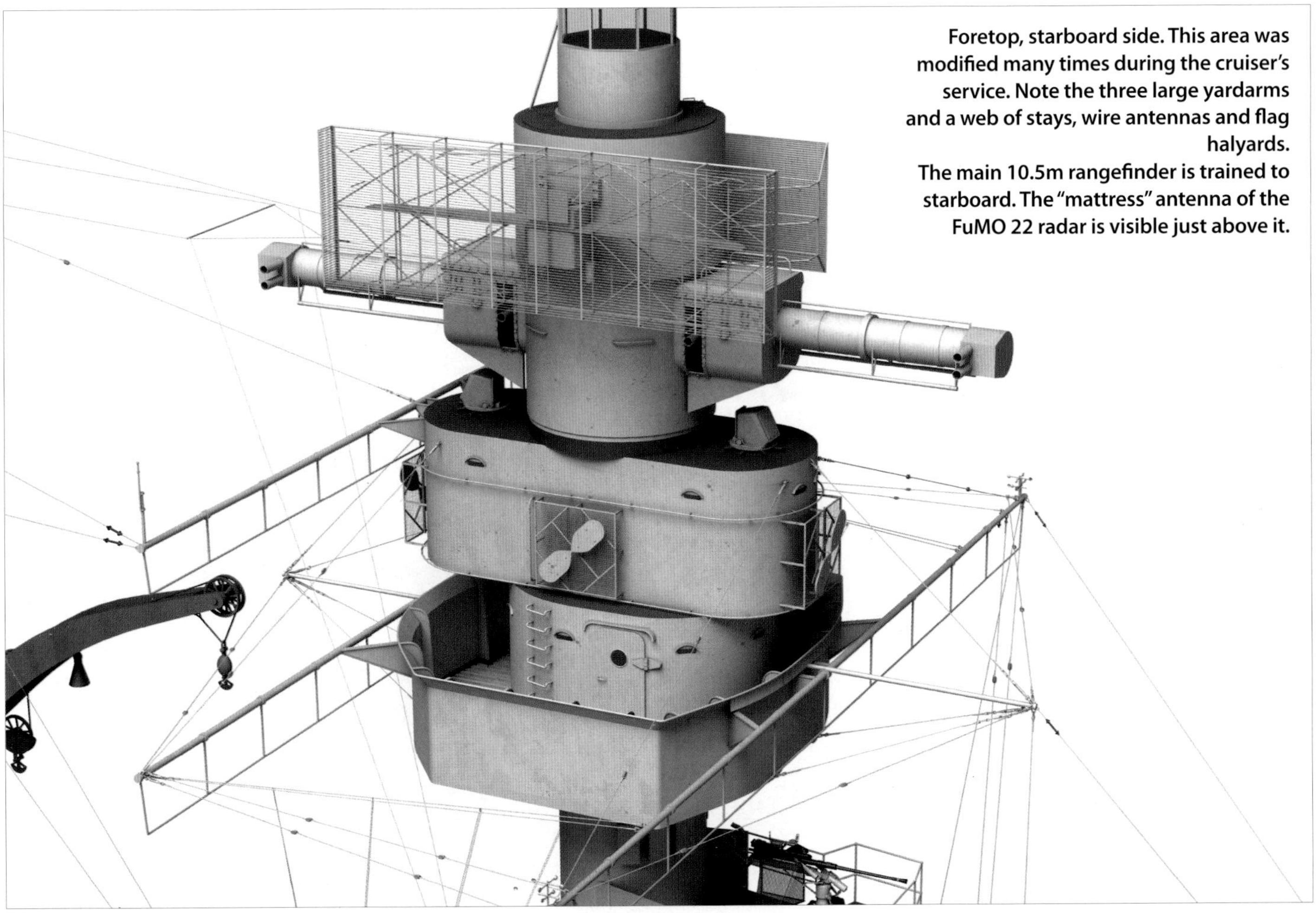

Foretop, starboard side. This area was modified many times during the cruiser's service. Note the three large yardarms and a web of stays, wire antennas and flag halyards.
The main 10.5m rangefinder is trained to starboard. The "mattress" antenna of the FuMO 22 radar is visible just above it.

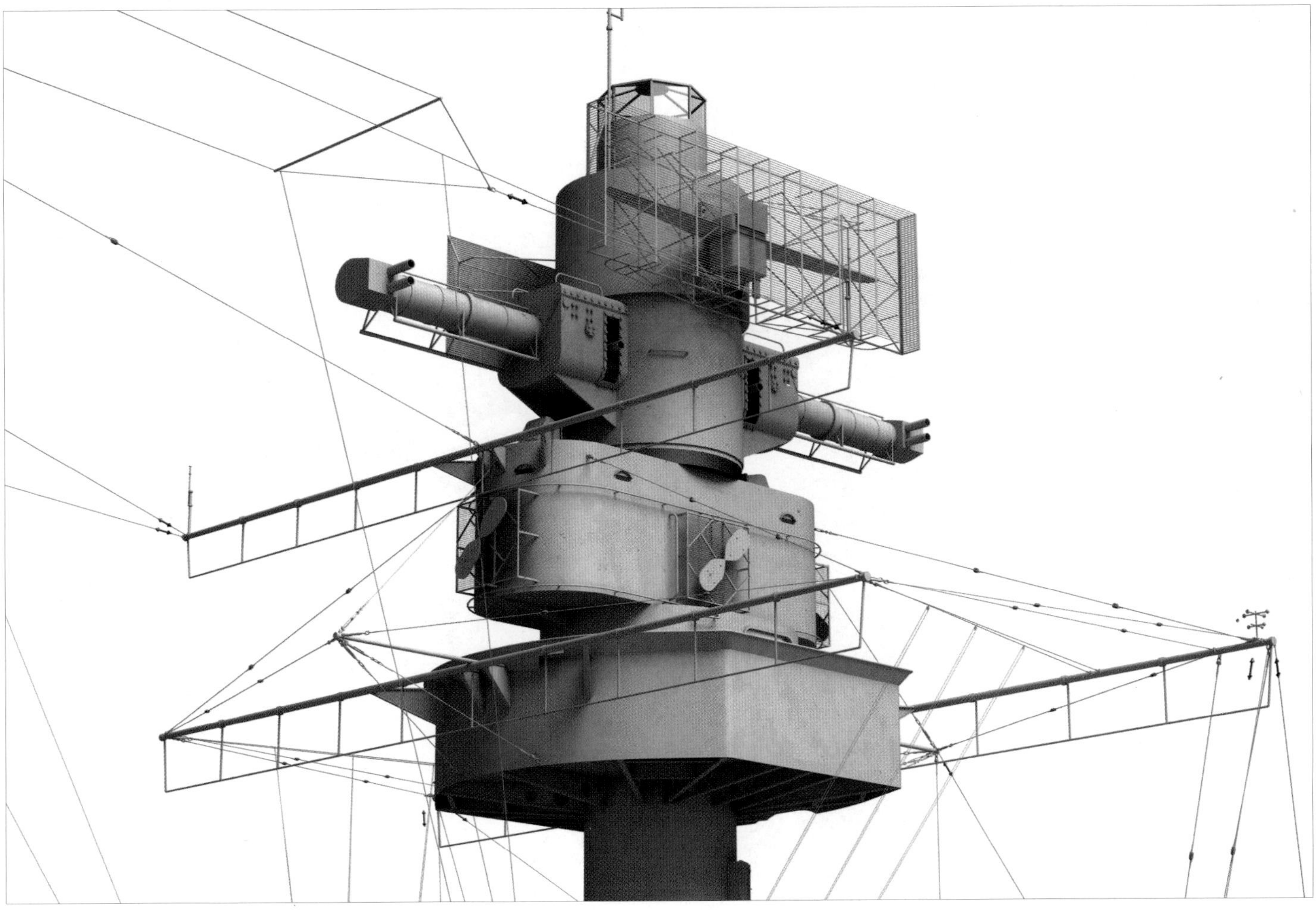

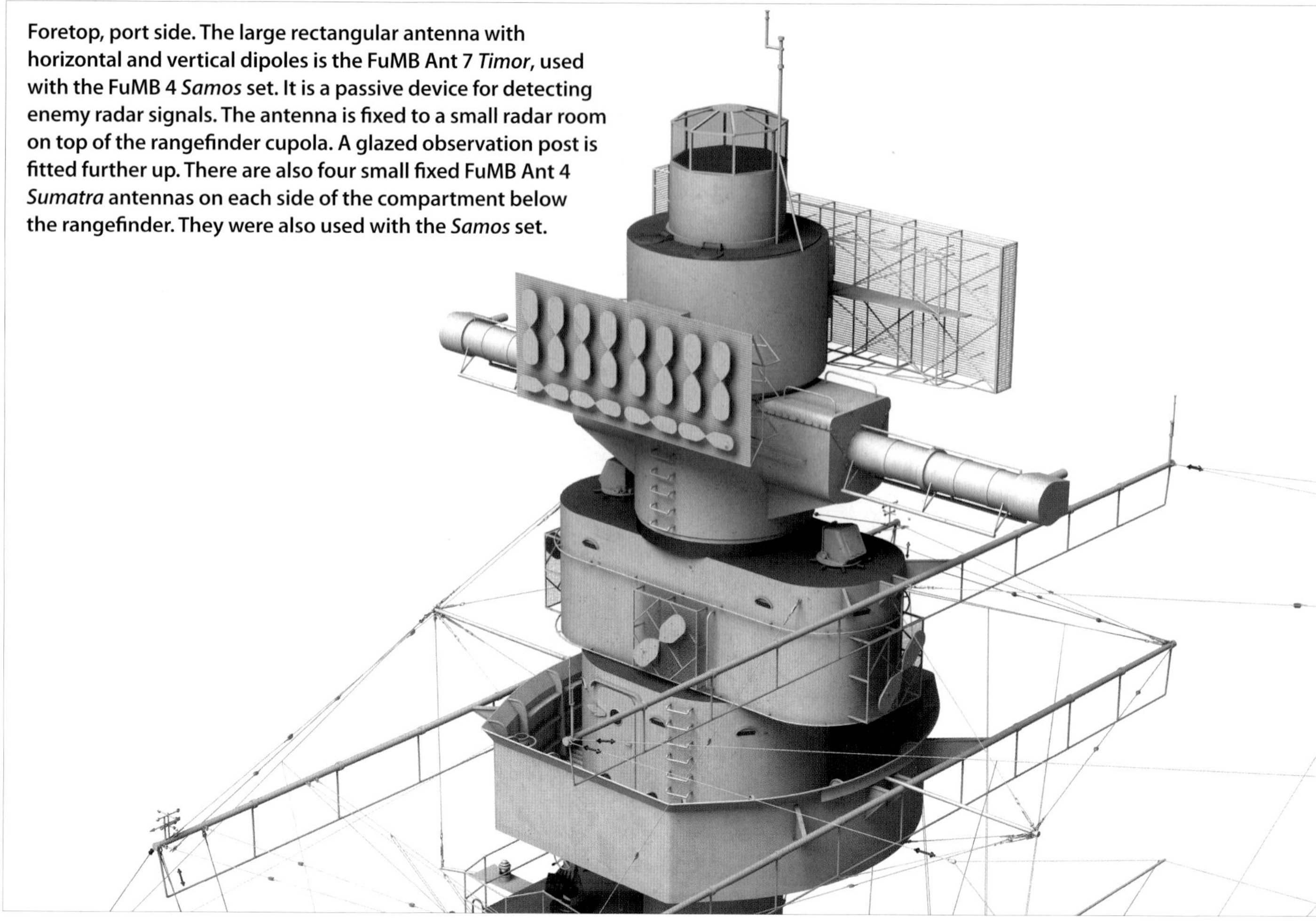

Foretop, port side. The large rectangular antenna with horizontal and vertical dipoles is the FuMB Ant 7 *Timor*, used with the FuMB 4 *Samos* set. It is a passive device for detecting enemy radar signals. The antenna is fixed to a small radar room on top of the rangefinder cupola. A glazed observation post is fitted further up. There are also four small fixed FuMB Ant 4 *Sumatra* antennas on each side of the compartment below the rangefinder. They were also used with the *Samos* set.

Overall views of the fore superstructure.

Forward pairs of 15cm L/55 C/28 guns. Anti-splinter plates reinforce the bottom front areas of the mounts. A small breakwater was added in front before the war to give better protection from spray. Life rafts are stowed on top of each mount.

The area around the catapult. A single motor launch is stowed on the starboard side; the port side deck is empty.

The ship's aircraft catapult with an Arado Ar-196 floatplane. The shipboard aircraft wore "T3+DH" markings.

It was only during Operation *Weserübung* in 1940 that the ship carried two aircraft on board, the second one being kept in the area behind the funnel. Note the Bordflieger Gruppe 196 emblem just behind the aircraft's engine (a seahorse against a blue background). The catapult has a small operator's platform on the left side.

One of the three twin heavy anti-aircraft artillery mounts on board. The 10.5cm L/65 C/33 guns replaced previous 8.8cm guns in 1940. The devices on the sides of the mounts are time fuse setters for the shells.

Starboard side crane. It was used to handle the ship's motorboats. A small operator's platform with control wheels can be seen.

Port side crane for handling the Ar-196 floatplane.

A searchlight platform on the funnel with four 150cm searchlights installed. Later in the war the forward pair was removed and the platform truncated.

The funnel as seen from the starboard side. The mainmast is fixed to its back.

The funnel as seen from the port side. The tall cap was fitted in the spring of 1942 and would remain unchanged until the sinking of the ship.

Transport boats stowed on both sides of the ship just behind the funnel. The compartment between them is used for stowage of life rafts.

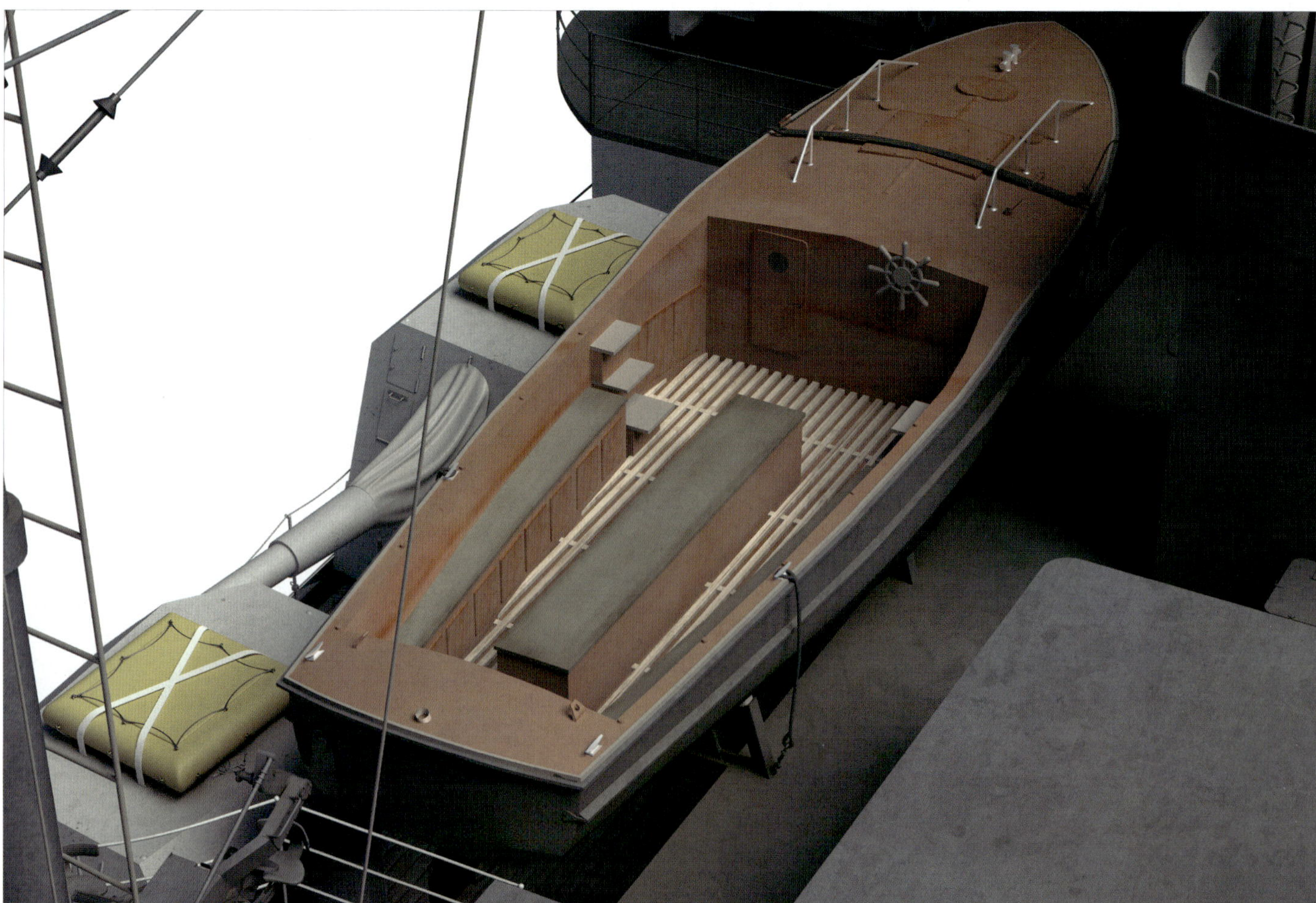

An SL-2 anti-aircraft artillery director behind the funnel.

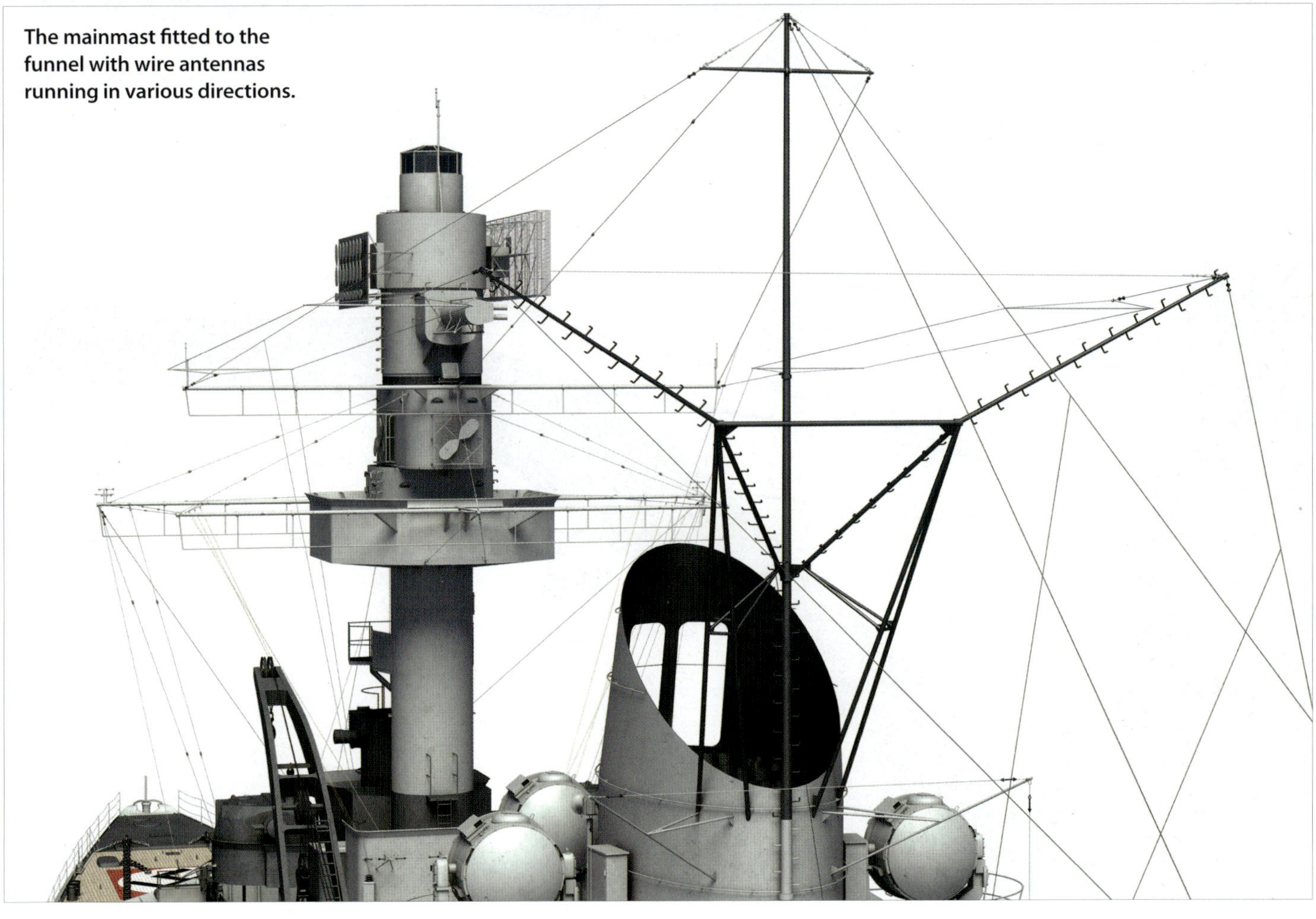

The mainmast fitted to the funnel with wire antennas running in various directions.

The arm of the starboard crane, resting on a special stand on the aft superstructure.

The curved arm of the port crane. It was normally positioned high above the deck and pointing forward.

Close-up views of the twin 3.7cm L/83 C/30 mount. Three seats for the crew are visible at the front. The right seat is for the elevation controller, the left one for the train controller, and the middle one is for the aimer/gunner. The mount is triaxially stabilized.

This mount was a standard AA weapon on Kriegsmarine ships at the beginning of the war. However, by 1942 it had become obsolete. Its low rate of fire (single shells were loaded manually) made the guns inefficient against fast moving targets.

The lower level of the aft superstructure. Additional "Vierlings" were installed here in 1942, replacing the single 2cm mounts. Their empty bases are visible near the quadruple mounts.

Row cutters with their davits fitted at both sides of the aft superstructure.

Overall views of the aft superstructure.

The aft command post with a 10.5m main artillery rangefinder. Both rangefinders were most often kept trained to one side by their crews.

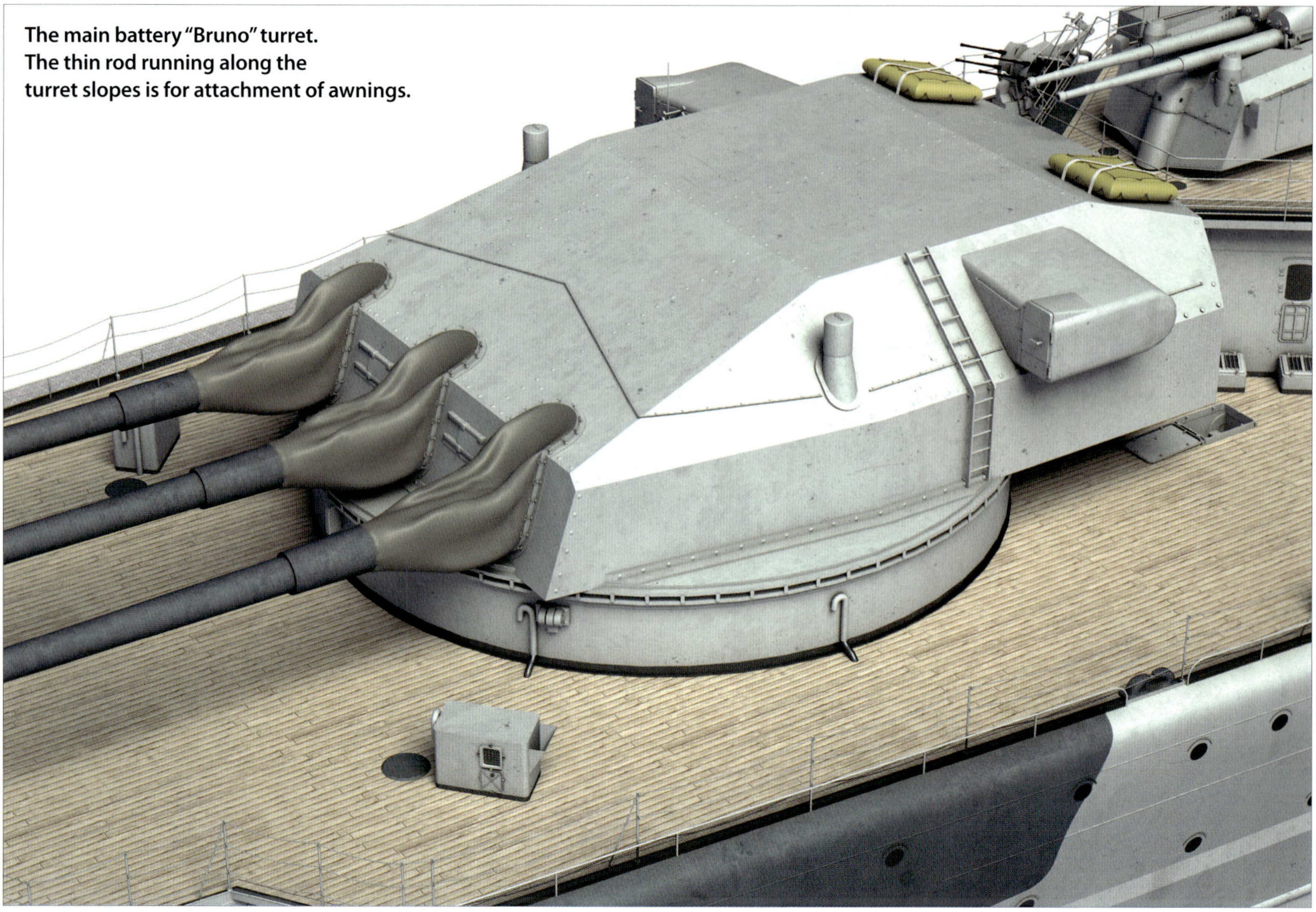

The main battery "Bruno" turret.
The thin rod running along the turret slopes is for attachment of awnings.

The area where the quarterdeck elevates to the main deck. Note the accommodation ladders stowed at the deck edges.

53.3cm quadruple torpedo launchers at the stern. These mounts were positioned very low above the waterline, which often made them inoperable in heavy weather. The shields had not been fitted when the ship was commissioned but they were installed shortly afterwards. A capstan for the stern anchor is visible between the mounts.

The cruiser's stern. Only the port side has an anchor. Also note the degaussing cables entering the hull close to the stern, the air recognition swastika and two single 2cm mounts just behind the torpedo tubes. The side rods which protect the propeller blades are in a stowed position.

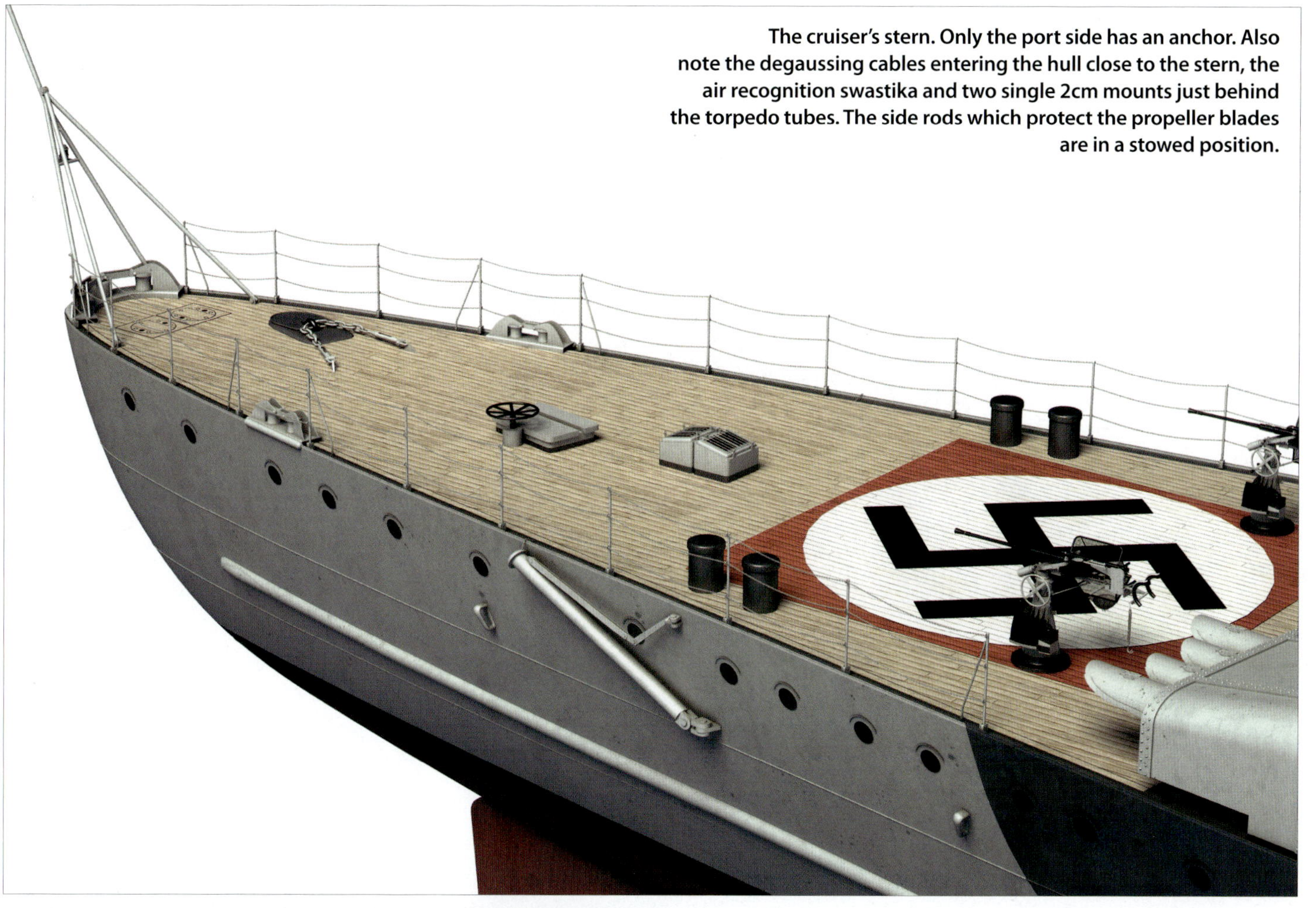

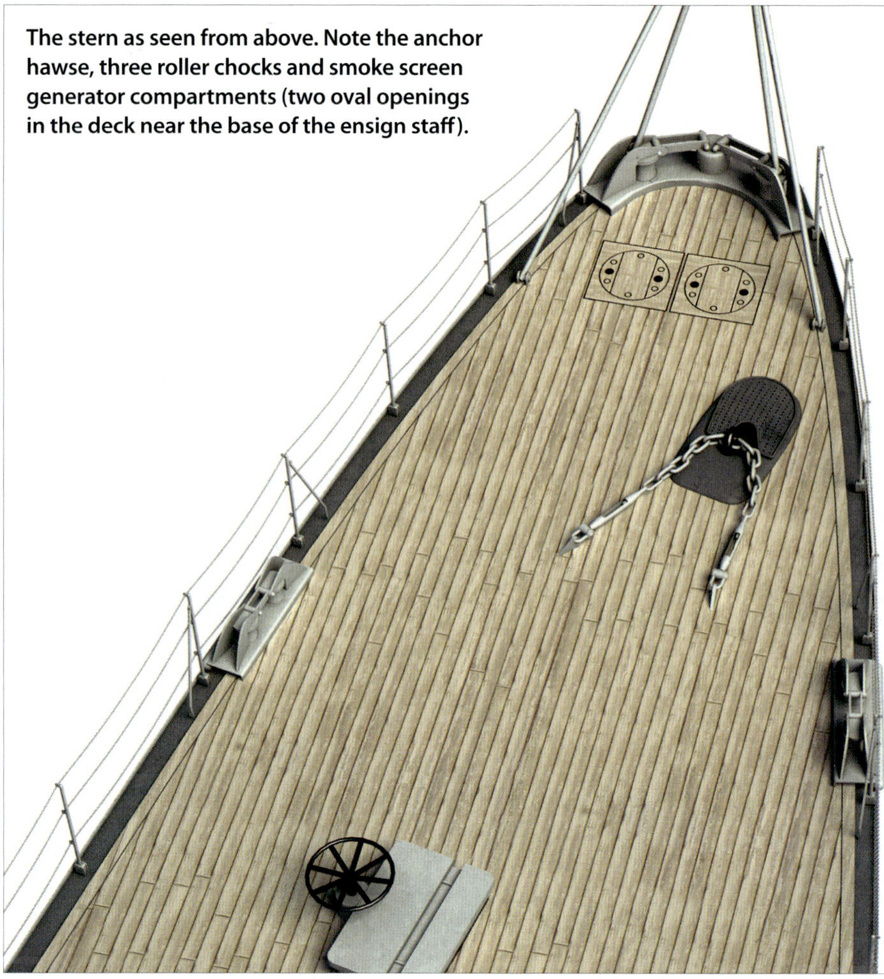

The stern as seen from above. Note the anchor hawse, three roller chocks and smoke screen generator compartments (two oval openings in the deck near the base of the ensign staff).

Germany's crest, the *Reichsadler*, was removed from the tip of the stern at the beginning of the war.

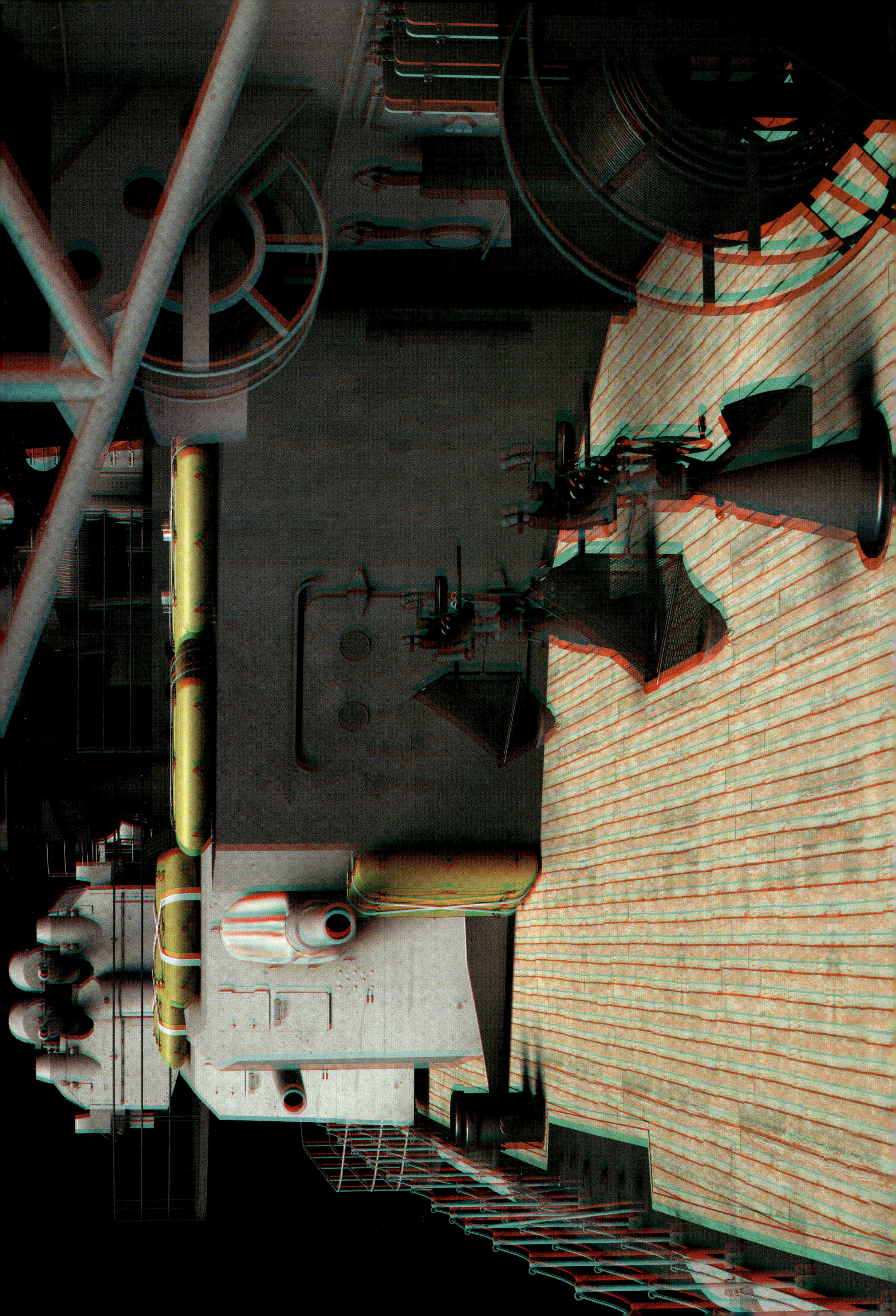

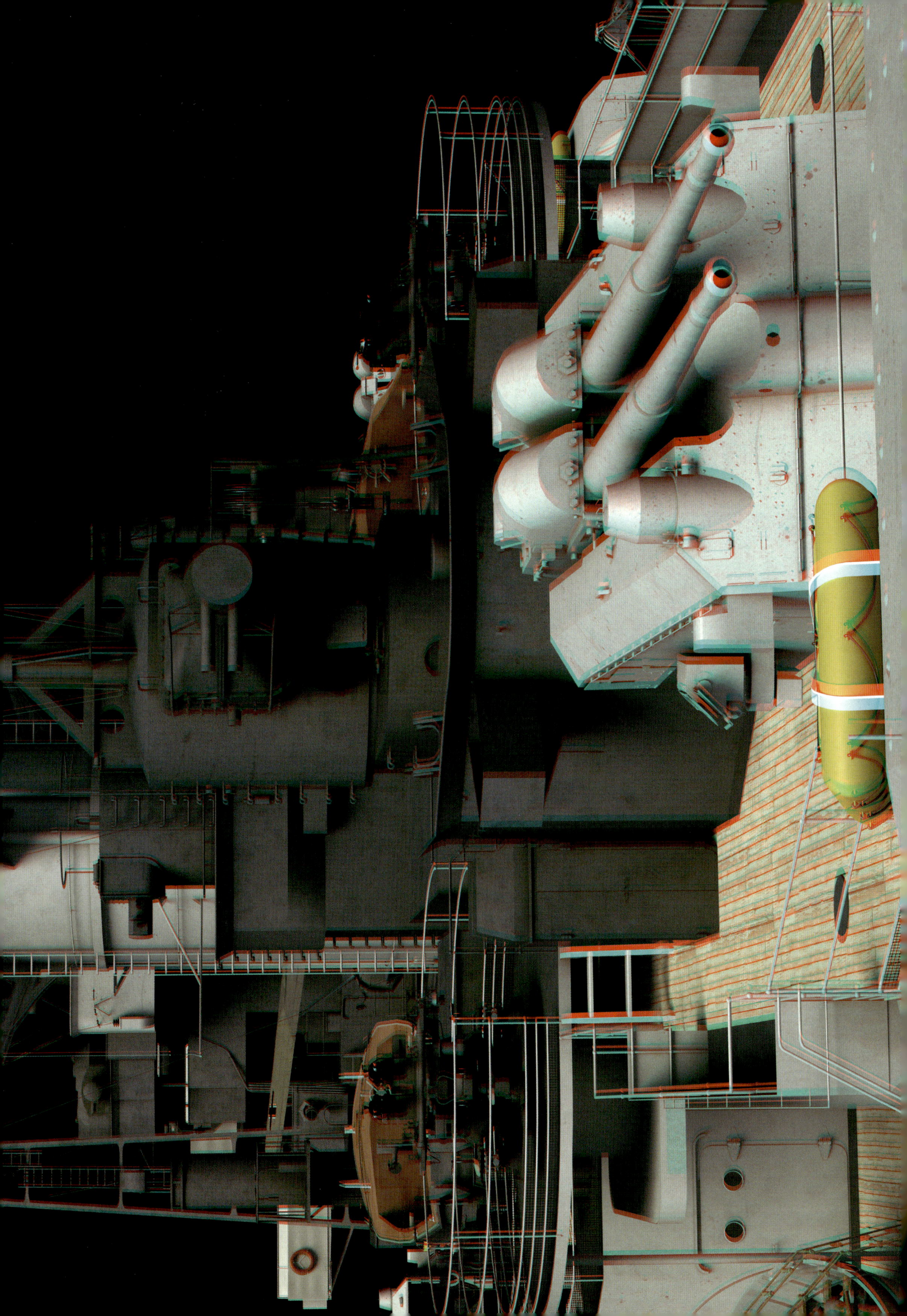

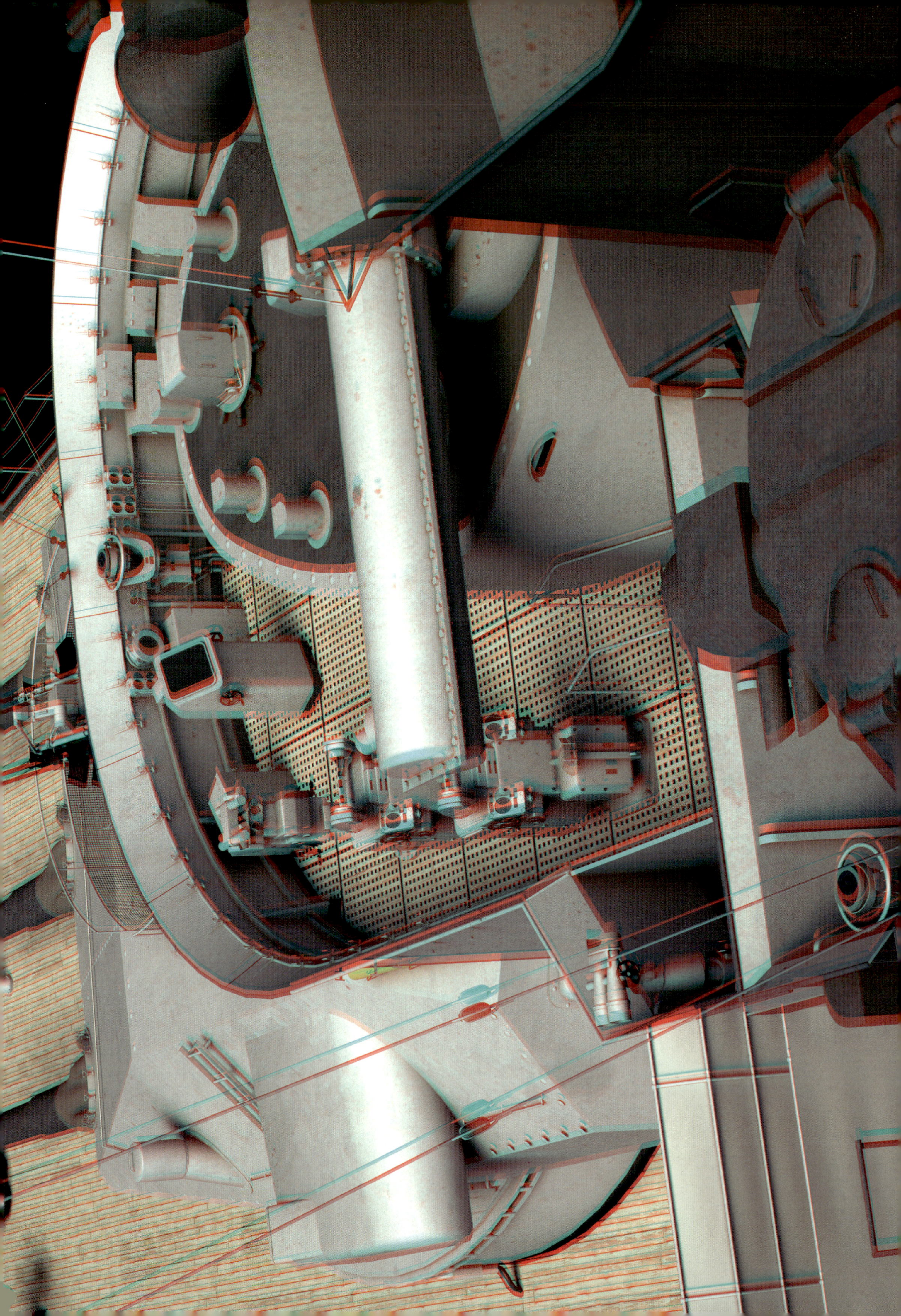

The Heavy Cruiser Lützow – Stefan Dramiński • LUBLIN 2014 • ISBN 978-83-64596-07-0

3D illustrations, text and captions: **Stefan Dramiński** • Translation: **Łukasz Prusza** • Design: **KAGERO STUDIO** – Marcin Wachowicz

Oficyna Wydawnicza KAGERO • www.kagero.pl • e-mail: kagero@kagero.pl, marketing@kagero.pl

Editorial office, Marketing, Distribution: Oficyna Wydawnicza KAGERO, Akacjowa 100, os. Borek, Turka, 20-258 Lublin 62, Poland, phone/fax (+48) 81 501 21 05

w w w . k a g e r o . p l